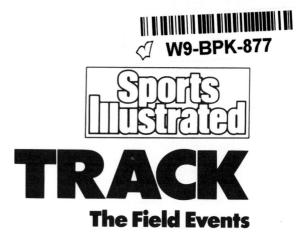

Sports Illustrated

TRACK

The Field Events

Sports Illustrated Winner's Circle Books

BOOKS ON TEAM SPORTS

Baseball
Basketball
Football: Winning Defense
Football: Winning Offense
Hockey
Lacrosse
Pitching
Soccer

BOOKS ON INDIVIDUAL SPORTS

Bowling
Competitive Swimming
Cross-Country Skiing
Figure Skating
Golf
Racquetball
Running for Women
Skiing
Tennis
Track: Championship Running
Track: The Field Events

SPECIAL BOOKS

Backpacking
Canoeing
Fly Fishing
Scuba Diving
Small-Boat Sailing
Strength Training
Training with Weights

TRACK
The Field Events

**by Jim Santos
and Ken Shannon**

Photography by Heinz Kluetmeier

Sports Illustrated
Winner's Circle Books
New York

My thanks to all the athletes who were so instrumental in my success as a coach: those boys and girls at Lebanon Union High School in Oregon, Bloom Township High School, Illinois, and at Cal State Hayward. Thanks to all the coaches who gave me their humor, hints, techniques, and support—coaches like Marcel Hetu, Don Chu, Steve Miller, Bill Vandenburgh, Sam Bell, and Fred Wilt. To my wife, Carolyn, a big thanks for all those years as a coach's wife, traveling with me from coast to coast, helping me with the meets, clinics, and athletes. Thanks to my daughter, Kelly, one of my best friends, and to my son, Dallas, a very Special Olympics athlete.

To Eunice Kennedy Shriver and Sargent Shriver: your inspiration has changed my life in sports.

And thanks to Ken Shannon for sharing this book with me.

—Jim Santos

Picture credits: For *Sports Illustrated:* Walter Iooss, Jr., pp. 3, 278; Ronald C. Modra, p. 42; Rich Clarkson, pp. 82, 150; John Dominis, p. 112; Warren Morgan, pp. 156, 204. Cover by John McDonough. All other photographs by Heinz Kluetmeier.

This book includes portions of *Sports Illustrated Track: Field Events* by Bobbie Moore and W. J. Bowerman (Philadelphia and New York: J. B. Lippincott Company, Copyright © 1977 by Time Inc. All rights reserved).

FIRST EDITION

Designer: Kim Llewellyn

Library of Congress Cataloging in Publication Data

Santos, Jim.
   Sports illustrated track : the field events / by Jim Santos and
Ken Shannon ; photography by Heinz Kluetmeier.
       p. cm. — (Sports illustrated Winners circle books)
   Summary: Techniques for achieving excellence in various track
events. Includes diet, exercises, and training.
   ISBN 0-452-26273-9
   1. Track-athletics—Juvenile literature.   [1. Track and field.]
I. Shannon, Ken.   II. Kluetmeier, Heinz. ill.   III. Title.
IV. Series.
GV1060.5.S26   1989
796.42—dc20   89-6110
91 92 93 94 95 AG/HL 10 9 8 7 6 5 4 3 2 1

Contents

THE THROWS

by Ken Shannon

10 | The Shot Put   185

11 | The Discus Throw   205

12 | The Javelin Throw   225

AFTERWORD

by Jim Santos and Ken Shannon

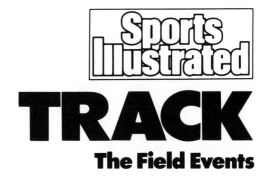

TRACK

The Field Events

Introduction

At a meet in Stockholm some years ago, a team of U.S. field-events competitors and a team of U.S. distance runners challenged each other in a 440 relay. The gun went off and the first field-events man, a burly discus thrower, was 5 yards down the track before the first distance man, a steeplechaser, got off his marks. Despite valiant efforts by the distance runners, the field-events men won easily. How could this happen?

The field-events athletes had two things going for them: explosiveness and sprinter's speed, crucial factors in all field events. Size and weight, while important, are not enough to make a good shot-putter. If you are agile, fast, and explosive, consider yourself qualified to try the shot or discus even if your size is only average.

In any of the field events, controlled strength is more valuable than mere bulk. Whether you are male or female* and whether you want to be a high jumper or a discus thrower, a good weight-lifting program should be an integral part of your training. We will not prescribe weight training programs for every event in this book, but with the help of your physical education department and the lifting exercises listed here, you should be able to tailor a program to your needs. Just remember never to lift weights without spotters and proper supervision.

In addition to strength, speed, and explosiveness, you need a good sense of timing. As you cross the shot-put ring or approach the high-jump bar, the different parts of your body must flow smoothly and in the right sequence, or all your strength and speed will be released at the wrong moment and the effort will be wasted.

---

*All the events covered in this book, except for the hammer throw and the pole vault, are open to both men and women. Where applicable, we have noted the differences in dimensions of implements.

All field events require of the athlete varying combinations of strength, speed, explosiveness, and power.

This is where technique comes in. Keep in mind that the techniques of the best field-events athletes will differ from each other and that there are no hard-and-fast rules. The best athletes have found things that work for them but may not necessarily work for you. The basics we describe here will give you a solid grounding in your event. Then you must learn to know yourself and your abilities. Become a student of your event. With time, experience, and fitness, you will be ready to experiment on your own.

Meanwhile, the main thing is to enjoy learning to get the most out of yourself, whatever your performance level.

THE JUMPS

by Jim Santos

1

The Principles of Jumping

There are four competitive jumping events—the pole vault, the high jump, the long jump, and the triple jump—and certain basic principles are inherent in all of them; only the method of leaving the ground differentiates the jumps. An athlete's ability to leave the ground at a given speed and at a specific angle are the two factors that separate the great jumpers from all the rest.

Should all jumpers have some basic speed? Yes. Must all jumpers be exceptionally fast? No. A jumper's ability to generate speed at the takeoff and to maintain good jumping technique through it is more important than blazing speed. For example, the long jumper who can hit the board at a good rate of speed and get into correct takeoff position will do much better than the jumper who is unusually fast but lacks good positioning technique at the takeoff. In general, being able to generate speed through the approach, into the takeoff, and off the takeoff foot is the key that can transform an average jumper into an exceptional one.

Agility is important for all jumpers—not just the vaulter, who must twist his body over the bar, but the triple jumper and high jumper as well. Once in the air, any jumper must be able to control his body in free flight, or all his previous effort will be wasted. Getting over the bar in the vault and the high jump, rotating the arms for extra distance in the long jump, and maintaining a good erect posture in the triple jump are all facets of the jumps that require sound technique and, ideally, a good dose of agility.

Since jumpers must leave the ground and get into the air for an extended period of time, power is also a must. Indeed, the ability of a jumper to spring forcefully, "exploding" off the ground, is so important that inches—and even feet—are often lost (or gained) at the moment when the foot leaves the ground or toeboard.

15

Will and motivation in a jumper often count as much as innate athletic ability.

Much has been written about the difference between fast-twitch and slow-twitch muscle fibers. Does the athlete have the necessary amount of fast-twitch muscle fibers to make him or her a good jumper? Or will an excess of slow-twitch fibers detract from the jumper's speed? Most athletes never undergo the muscle biopsy test necessary to answer that question, but there are other ways to determine jumping ability. Many coaches rely on basic jumping and running tests, but no tests are infallible. If you have the will and motivation to be a good jumper, you can channel those energies into developing greater speed and better technique, no matter what a jumping or running test initially tells you.

Depending upon the event, a jumper measures his success either by how far or by how high he jumps. Success is a personal matter, and if you decide to get serious about jumping, you must learn what a good jump is for you. For example, if you pole-vault 14 feet in a competition one day and it's a personal best, you should feel good about that, whether you win the competition or not. Personal achievement is the basic goal for all athletes and for all coaches working with those athletes. To win a gold medal is great, but personal achievement is paramount.

That brings us to the all-important issue of an athlete's mental attitude. Is it better to have a stable, easygoing outlook on your event and the competition, or should you have that "killer instinct"?

In many cases, the killer instinct in a young athlete does just that: it kills the athlete's performance. But if you can control that instinct and use its energy and emotion as a positive motivating force, you will elevate your performance level and jump to heights or distances greater than you might ever have dreamed possible.

As an athlete in track and field, you must believe that you can succeed in your event. If you don't, you will never be able to develop a set of goals worthy of your time and effort. It's far better to say to yourself, "I'd sure like to be able to long-jump 20 feet this season" than to say "I'll never be able to jump that far." By stating a precise desire in a positive way, you give yourself something to shoot for. By denying yourself 20 feet as a jumper, you deny yourself what may be an attainable goal. Worse, you acknowledge a fundamental lack of confidence, which for any athlete is unacceptable.

Instead of thinking "I can't," think of how you are going to react when you land in the sand at 20 feet 1 inch, a personal best. Will you jump for joy? Raise your arms in victory? Clap your hands in happiness? How, precisely, will you react at that moment of personal triumph? For that matter, can you imagine what your jump will look like as you leave the board and sail more than 20 feet out into the sand?

These types of positive images can help any athlete attain a better performance level, and it's the purpose of this book to show you how you can do it, too. In all my years of coaching—from junior-high and high school beginners to college athletes and world-class Olympians—I have found that all competitive jumpers possess four fundamental qualities: good technique, strength, speed, and a positive mental attitude. Becoming a jumper is not easy. It takes time, patience, and know-how. But if you approach the jumping events with a positive mental attitude, the other three fundamental qualities are attainable.

The ideas about jumping that I share with you in this book have been refined over a period of years by myself and by other coaches and athletes in track and field around the world. There's nothing magical about them. You can make them work for you, as long as you're willing to put in the necessary effort.

You do have your work cut out for you if you want to be a quality jumper, but believe me, it's healthy work and its benefits—physical, psychological, and social—can last a lifetime.

So, let's suit ourselves up and get started.

2

Plyometric Training for the Field Events

Plyometric training is designed to stimulate the reactive properties of muscles—that is, their ability to respond quickly to different degrees of flexing or contracting. Track people have found that sound reactive capabilities in key muscles are crucial for success in the jumps, as well as in the throws and sprints. Plyometric training not only strengthens the appropriate muscles for the jumps (primarily the legs and arms), it also trains them to respond faster and more powerfully at the moment of takeoff. The effect, as we'll see, of a stronger, faster, more powerful takeoff is a longer or higher jump.

Plyometrics has often been called the "bounce-load" method of training because the athlete literally trains the muscles to bounce and load up with neuromuscular energy for the actual jump. Such bouncing and loading occurs, for example, when a high jumper plants his takeoff foot for the jump. As the foot touches the ground, the jumper lets his knee and ankle flex slightly, which is similar to a bounce. Plyometrics coaches call this "loading" the leg. Next, the jumper must sense when to stop the loading phase, maintain his weight and force on the leg, and then return all of these energies up his leg and to the rest of his body on the takeoff. This is called "unloading" the leg, and the entire process is similar to bouncing a rubber ball on a gym floor. The harder a ball is thrown or bounced on the floor, the harder and faster it will rebound because of the "loading" and "unloading" effect on the ball. It shouldn't take a degree in physics for us to see that the faster the ball can leave the floor, the higher it will bounce. Similarly, the faster and harder a jumper can load and unload his takeoff leg, the higher (or farther) he will jump.

During the loading phase of a jump, when the takeoff foot touches down and there is a slight shock-absorbing flexion of the takeoff knee and ankle, the extensor muscles of the takeoff leg load and stretch in what is known as an

19

Plyometric training can help you improve your leg strength and leg speed for the jumps.

20   *eccentric contraction.* The next phase of the jump involves the tightening or shortening of the jumping muscles into what is known as a *concentric contraction.* This is the pushing phase of the jump, when the muscles convert the energy stored during the eccentric phase, and with it propel the body upward or outward. As any jumper will tell you, this concentric phase must be forceful and explosive. Through plyometric training, a jumper can train these muscles to react quickly and forcefully for a strong pushing movement into the jump.

Another example of these quick, powerful eccentric-concentric contractions can be seen when a player jumps to make a block in volleyball. The player jumps off both feet by dropping his weight down quickly (the loading, or eccentric, phase of the jump), then leaping into the air as fast and as high as possible (the unloading, or concentric, phase). Similar loading-unloading movements occur during the jump ball in basketball, and in the windups (or approaches) and releases in the discus, shot, javelin, and hammer throwing events in track and field.

For all these sports, and for many others, a training program that incorporates a regular schedule of plyometric exercises can pay great dividends. If you decide to include plyometric training in your jumping or throwing program, a word of caution: Avoid wearing hand weights, ankle weights, weighted vests, or weight jackets while performing *any* plyometric exercise. The reason for this is simple. In order to train your muscles to react quickly, you must exercise them at a high rate of speed. Placing weights on the arms, legs, or torso slows your rate of movement considerably; as a consequence, the plyometric exercise has little value. If you perform plyometric exercises while wearing weights, your muscles may become stronger, but they will lack the speed necessary for a good response during a jump (or as you will see in the second section, a throw). In addition, you run the risk of injuring the areas of the body you are weighting.

As we go on, we'll cover training techniques geared for each specific event. For now, here are some basic plyometric exercises that can be used to good result by any jumper.

THE EXERCISES

Skips

Skipping is the same exercise you used to do as a child, consisting of an alternating hop-step movement in which you can emphasize either height or distance. If you are a long jumper or a triple jumper, concentrate mostly on skipping for distance. If you are a high jumper or vaulter, skip more for height. A good skipping workout for a beginning jumper might include:

1. Skip for 30 meters without raising the knees much. Repeat 3 times.
2. Skip for 30 meters, raising the knees about halfway. Repeat 3 times.
3. Skip for 30 meters with the knees at waist level. Repeat 3 times.
4. Skip for 50 meters with exaggerated arm and knee action (that is, bring the upper leg higher than parallel to the ground, and swing the arms above the head). Repeat 3 times.
5. Skip for 50 meters, jumping as high as possible on the skips. Repeat 3 times.

Bounds

From a crouched position with your arms at your side, leap up and forward. While you are in the air, kick your buttocks with your heels. When you land, go immediately into another bound.

Bounding forward like this is a good exercise for developing rebound strength in your legs—that is, your ability to land and then jump again with great speed and strength. Bounds can be done on both legs, or on one leg at a time, alternating legs.

Alternate Leg Bounds

Alternate leg bounds are like taking giant steps in the air. To do them, walk a few steps; then push off with one leg and land on the opposite leg. Move your arms forward and back like a triple jumper (more on triple jumping later). Keep your front knee up and your opposite leg back while you are in the air. Bound for 30 meters, alternating legs on each bound. (Note: there is no step or skip between bounds.) Repeat 3 to 5 times, resting, as necessary, between sets.

Like skipping, alternate leg bounds are an exhilarating form of exercise which prepares the muscles of the leg for quick yet painless loading and unloading—one of the keys to success in the jumps.

Skipping and Bounding

Shown here are basic skipping and bounding exercises. For a complete skipping/bounding workout, vary your arm and knee action.

Bounding with an erect posture and double-arm action.

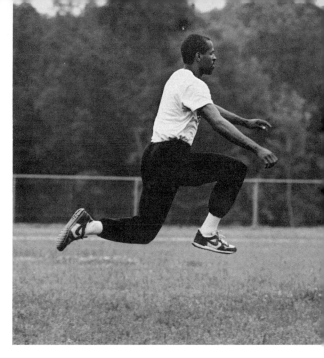

Skipping with knees at waist level.

Alternate leg bounds.

To do alternate leg bounds, walk a few steps, then push off with one leg (A) and land on the other (B). Keep your front knee up and your opposite leg back as you bound along, maintaining an erect posture.

A   B

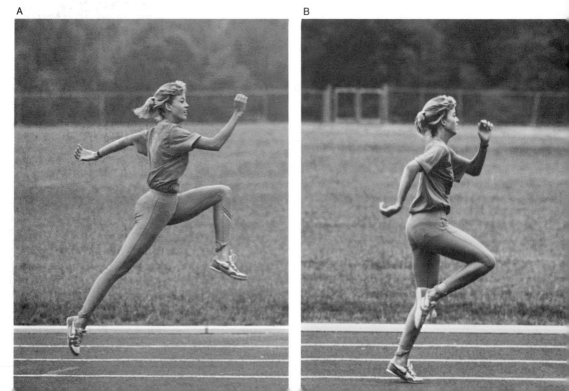

Hops

If you're a beginning jumper, start by hopping on both legs (double leg hops), and once your body is accustomed to the movement, try hopping on one leg (single leg hops). You can hop in place, or you can hop for distance. When you do hops, try to kick your buttocks with the heel of your hopping foot (or feet). Track people call that an *active* hopping motion. Here are some hints that can help you develop your legs and body position:

- Keep your back erect.
- Do not lean forward when hopping.
- Land almost flat-footed, not on the heels or balls of your feet.
- Work on grass or a soft surface, such as a gymnastics mat, when starting.
- Move your arms in a swinging motion in order to develop explosive strength in your legs.

Drills for Hopping

1. Standing erect, hop in place 10 times, kicking your buttocks with your heels.
2. Standing erect, hop in place 10 times, bringing your knees in front of your chest. Rest. Repeat.
3. Do double leg hops for 20 meters, kicking your buttocks with your heels. Repeat 3 times.
4. Do double leg hops for 30 meters, kicking your buttocks with your heels. Repeat 3 times.
5. Do single leg hops (right leg) for 20 meters, kicking your right buttock with your right heel. Repeat 3 times.
6. Do single leg hops (left leg) for 20 meters, kicking your left buttock with your left heel. Repeat 3 times.
7. Set out 20 12-inch-high parking cones a yard apart, in a straight line. Do a double leg hop over each cone. Repeat 3 times.
8. Do a single leg hop over each cone: first the right leg (3 sets), and then the left leg (3 sets).
9. If you are a high jumper, jump for height over each of the cones. If you are a triple jumper, vaulter, or long jumper, increase the space between the cones to 1½ yards, then to 2 yards, as the season progresses; jump for speed between the cones. Repeat 3 times.

Hopping

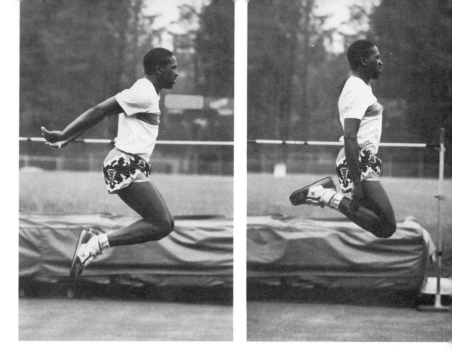

Hopping in place, kicking buttocks with heels.

Double-leg hops, kicking buttocks with heels.

Leaps

Leaps are strenuous and difficult, but wonderfully beneficial. Imagine that you are a basketball player leaping for a rebound. Start in a low position, with your buttocks almost level with your knees. Keep your back erect and your head up, looking straight ahead. Leap straight up into the air, letting your legs simply hang straight. Leap in the air 10 times, rest 30 seconds, and repeat for a total of 3 sets (30 leaps).

Next, drop down to a medium-low position, with your buttocks higher than your knees. Leap into the air 10 times, rest 30 seconds, and repeat for a total of 3 sets (30 leaps). Leap as fast as you can.

Ricochets

Hop as quickly as you can, lifting both feet together. Set small (2- by 4-inch) blocks 2 feet apart over a distance of 10 yards. Hop as quickly as you can over the blocks. The idea is to keep the touchdowns quick and light, the forward

Plyometric box drills.
Place three to five sturdy wooden boxes of different heights in a row as shown. Starting from a half-crouched position on the ground (A), leap quickly onto the first box, bringing your heels to your buttocks (B, C, D), then down onto the ground (E, F), then up onto the next

A   B   C

movement continuous. Ricochets are a great plyometric exercise for building up quickness and speed. Use short, quick arm movements.

Box Drills

Hop over rows of three or more boxes that range from 8 inches to 18 inches high. By varying the order of boxes of different heights and by hopping both forward and from side to side, you can create a challenging and fun range of exercises.

The Leap Box Drill

Place four or five sturdy wooden boxes 3 to 6 feet apart. From a half-crouched position on the ground, leap up onto the first box, then down to the ground, and leap up quickly to the next box. Continue this drill until you have completed jumps onto all the boxes. Then do a set jumping over the boxes.

The leap box drill is a good exercise for developing strength and speed in the legs. Repeat this drill 8 to 10 times.

box, and so on, until you have completed jumps on all the boxes. Maintain good posture. You can vary this exercise by jumping over the boxes.

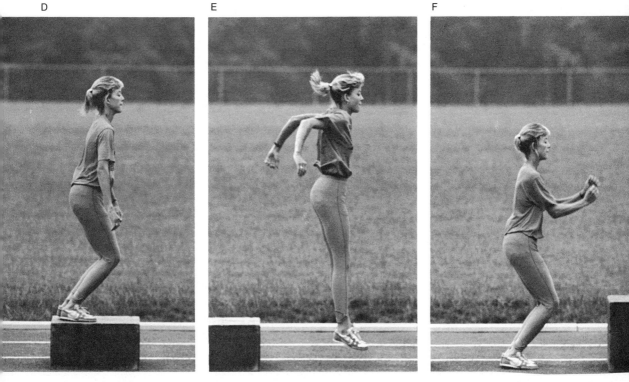

D E F

The Scissor Jump Drill

Start in a split position, with one leg forward and one leg back. Jump straight up into the air, switch legs, land, and explode back. Raise your arms as you jump to improve your lift. This exercise is excellent for developing strong muscles in the buttocks, hips, and thighs. Do 10 scissor jumps, rest 30 seconds, and repeat twice for a total of 30 jumps.

Medicine Ball or Plyoball Exercises

We have all seen the traditional leather-covered medicine balls; they have been used extensively in sports training for years. Now there's a new device—a somewhat smaller ball that offers a greater range of exercises. It is known as a Plyoball (for its plyometric exercise value). The ball has several unique features:

1. It is soft, squeezable, and comes in a variety of weights, from 2 to 12 pounds.
2. It is approximately the size of a volleyball, which makes it far easier to handle than a traditional large medicine ball.
3. When used as a warm-up or exercise device, it maximizes the effectiveness of low-impact aerobics.
4. It floats, which is a big help if you want to train in a pool (something more and more track athletes are incorporating into their training programs).
5. It will improve your training by adding resistance to your workout.
6. It is fun and safe to use.

Plyoball tosses can also be performed with a traditional rubber or leather medicine ball. Whichever type you choose, use balls weighing from 5 to 15 pounds, depending upon your strength and development. (See the guidelines on page 41.)

Basic Plyoball and Medicine Ball Exercises for the Track and Field Athlete

Working with your coach, develop a regimen of Plyoball and medicine ball exercises from among those shown here to help develop your upper-body strength, flexibility, muscle quickness, and power. Do 3 sets of 10 repetitions each, resting for 30 seconds after each set. As the season progresses, increase the number of sets to 5, and increase the speed of the exercises.

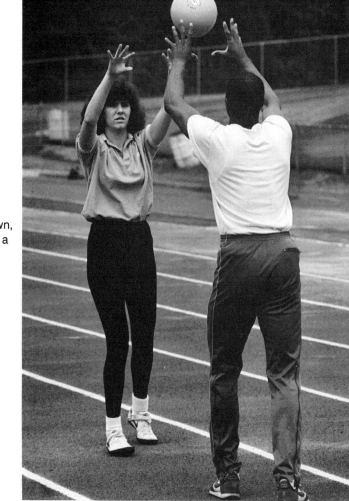

The overhand toss.
Set one foot forward slightly, as shown, and toss the ball back and forth with a partner, using a quick, brisk tossing motion.

A

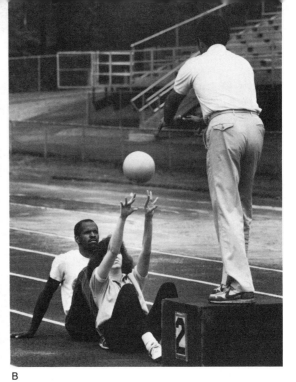

B

The incline two-handed toss.

Sit on the ground with a training partner behind you, supporting your back with his knees as shown. Another partner, standing on a sturdy box, now tosses you the Plyoball. You catch it in front of your chest (A), and toss it back, using a two-handed push-pass motion (B).

A

To increase your tossing effort, have your training partner stand on a box.

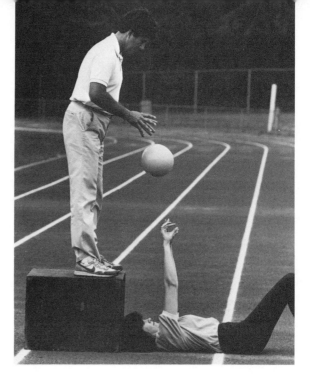

The prone two-handed toss.

Lie with your back on the ground, knees up, as shown. Your partner now drops the Plyoball into your outstretched hands (A), and you toss it back to him, using the two-handed push-pass motion (B, C).

B

C

A   B

The sit-up toss.

In this exercise, you sit on the ground and your training partner grasps your ankles. Your coach tosses the Plyoball to your hands, which are outstretched over your head (A). Keeping the ball over your head, bend back at the waist, touch the ball to the ground behind your head (B), perform a sit-up (C), and at the end of it, using an overhead motion, toss the ball back to your coach (D).

C

D

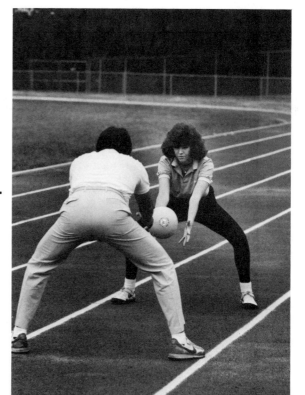

The underhand Plyoball toss.
Note the leg and upper-body
position. Stand 10 to 12 feet
apart. Keep the tosses brisk
and light. As the season
progresses, increase the
distance the ball is tossed.

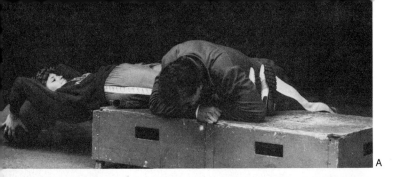

A

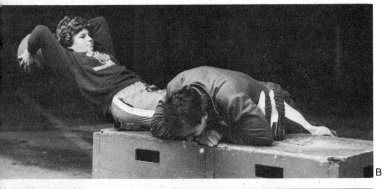

B

Variation on the sit-up toss.
In this variation, you sit on a low
double box, your legs straight out
in front. Your training partner
places his weight firmly but gently
over your knees, and you make
the two-handed overhead toss
after touching the ball to the floor.
Performing the sit-up on the box
increases your back's range of
motion, but be careful when performing this or any other back
extension exercise. To avoid back
injury, work with a light Plyoball
and keep your movements smooth
and fluid, not tense and jerky.

C

D

The Plyoball back-extension toss.

This is another exercise that should be done carefully, using a light Plyoball or medicine ball (4 to 6 pounds) for beginners. Lie face down across two boxes as shown, with your upper body extending beyond them. Your training partner gently places her weight over your legs, and as you perform a back extension, your coach tosses the Plyoball to you (A). You should catch the ball at full extension, then toss the ball back, using an overhand throwing motion (B, C, D). Again, do this one carefully!

A

B

C

D

A   B   C

Plyoball or medicine ball toss for throwers.
With its exaggerated stepping motion, this toss is especially useful for javelin throwers. The toss is made, upward and outward, at head level and to one side. Perform the exercise from both left and right sides. You can also perform this exercise kneeling on one leg, with the other leg forward.

The kneeling side toss.
In this exercise, you kneel and toss the ball with two hands from the side, at waist level. You can also perform this exercise standing.

A

B

C

A   B   C

The squat-leap-and-toss.
The name says it all. With the ball in front of you, squat, lift the ball, and leap straight up off your feet, pushing the ball with two hands overhead as you leap upward. Catch the ball and repeat.

The over-the-head toss.
Start in a half squat (A), and keeping your arms straight, toss the ball behind you, over your head, as you leap up (B, C). Try to follow through to achieve maximum lower back extension.

D

A

B

C

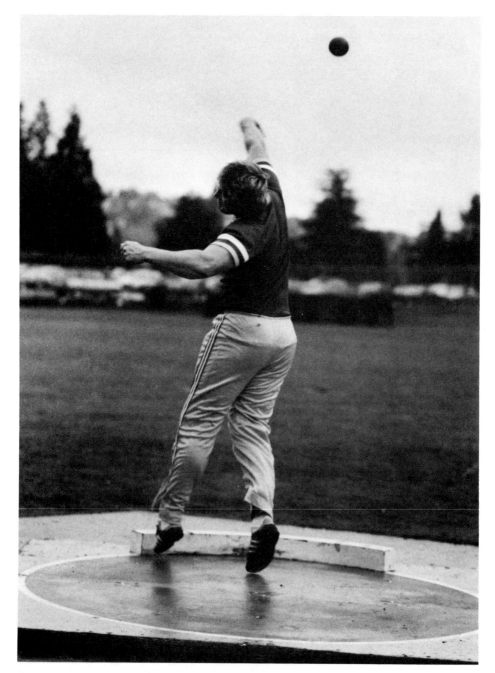

Throwing exercises can help shot putters and other throwers develop the explosive power they need for greater throwing distance.

GUIDELINES FOR DOING PLYOMETRIC EXERCISES

1. Be sure to have at least 4 weeks of solid weight training behind you before you start any plyometric exercises (see Chapter 9).

2. Start each workout with a good warm-up by jogging for at least 5 minutes, then stretching for 20 minutes. After a plyometric workout, jog again for 2 to 3 minutes; then do some acceleration runs for 30 to 40 meters.

3. Start any plyometric exercise at a moderate tempo but with an explosive movement; then increase the intensity as the repetitions increase. The faster you can move your legs or arms, the more effective the exercise will be.

4. Do the exercises in repetitions of 8 to 10 at a time. If you choose to do fewer reps, make sure each requires more exertion than usual.

5. Do no more than 3 or 4 sets at a time, depending on your development. Start with 2 sets of 10 reps, and as you develop more speed and strength, increase to 3 sets, then 4.

You will find that plyometric training will improve your cardiovascular fitness. This will allow you to work over a longer period of time and at a higher intensity rate as the season progresses. Plyometrics are fun, challenging, and pay great dividends. If you are preparing for a league or district meet near the end of the season, reduce the plyometric training to just once a week during the 3 weeks before the championship meet. For the last 2 weeks prior to the meet, do only light skips and bounds for tune-ups, but no heavy or intense work. This will allow your muscles to recover for better strength and performance.

If you have a district or state meet in the weeks following the league meet, do easy plyometrics for only one workout per week, and do them early in the week.

Use your imagination. Work with your coach and teammates in dreaming up new ideas for using the Plyoball or medicine ball. How far can you skip? How far can you bound? How fast can you skip for 100 meters on the grass? These are just a few of the ideas you can incorporate into any plyometric workout to make it fun, productive, and challenging. Plyometrics work. Include them in your training program and watch your progress. You'll be surprised by the results.

Now let's take a look at the jumping events themselves.

3

The Pole Vault

The pole vault is one of the most exciting events in track and field. Watching vaulters "sky" over the bar and literally fly into the air is a thrill that draws the attention of spectator and competitor alike.

Success in the pole vault really depends upon the action between the vaulter and the pole. The more experienced you are with the pole, and the better the pole is for your particular build and vaulting technique, the better your performance will be and the higher you will vault. No two pole vaulters are exactly the same, but all good vaulters have good running speed, strong gymnastic ability, and the physical and mental toughness to work hard over a long period of time. Perhaps the most important factor behind a pole vaulter's success is his ability to run fast and generate a lot of speed on the takeoff. Running speed allows you to transfer power into the pole when you plant it at the end of the approach; the power is returned to you when the pole straightens as you go into the vault. If you are slow, you will find it difficult to improve beyond a certain point, as you won't be able to bend the pole very much. However, if you are fast and can reach high on the plant and on the pole (more on this in a moment), you will be able to bend the pole back far enough for the power stored by the pole's bending to help propel you over the bar.

When you watch a top high school or collegiate vaulter, you will often see him reach for a heavier or stiffer pole as the bar is raised to a greater height. The vaulter knows that if, by running harder and faster, he can transfer enough energy into it, the stronger or stiffer pole will give him greater thrust over the bar.

How do you go about being able to use a heavier or stiffer pole? By getting stronger, running faster, and developing your vaulting technique so that you can use your talents in concert with the pole. Of course, your attitude will affect

43

Courage, strength, speed, agility, and mental toughness
are all requisites for being an outstanding pole vaulter.

all of these qualities, and just how far you can develop them is up to you as a person as much as as a vaulter. If you are tempted to take some shortcuts every now and then, you will find that your progress will also be cut. If you want to understand the technique of the vault, you must be willing to study the event, just as you would study any subject in school!. There is no shortcut to learning to pole-vault. The less you know about the pole vault, the less information you can use to help yourself in a practice or in a meet. Not studying the event means that you are not giving yourself a chance to develop as completely as you can.

GETTING STARTED IN THE POLE VAULT

When you first start learning to vault, the most important thing to remember is to land safely in a good landing pit. Do not vault into sand, sawdust, or any landing surface other than a foam rubber vaulting pit at least 14 feet long, 16 feet wide, and 2½ feet thick. Next, select a lightweight fiberglass pole that is not too long. For beginners I recommend a 12-foot pole, but if that seems too long, try a training pole, which is even shorter.

The Plant-and-Swing Drill

In this drill, you hold the pole almost parallel to the ground and about 8 to 9 feet up from the bottom, as shown, and make a four-step approach to the vault box (A). As you plant the pole, your coach should seize it (B) and assist your forward momentum as you draw

A B

For your first attempt, start by standing erect and holding the pole verti-cally directly in front of you. Now extend your right hand as high as possible up the length of the pole. This grip will allow you to control yourself through your earliest vaults and will prepare you for gripping the pole even higher. As a general rule, a beginner should grip the pole with his right hand 7 to 7½ feet up from the bottom, his left hand a little more than shoulder width apart from the right. When the pole is lifted to the horizontal, the right hand should be palm up, the left hand palm down. (Of course, if you're left-handed you should make your left hand the top hand, in which case it should be facing up when the pole is lifted to the horizontal, and the right hand should be facing down.)

Besides the landing pit and the bar, the vaulting area includes an approach track (anywhere from 140 to 175 feet long), at the end of which is a wedge-shaped indentation, called the vault box, into which the pole is planted. To get started in the vault, work without a bar in place, and stand back from the box so that your approach to it requires only four quick steps (about 14 or 15 feet back from the box). Hold the pole in front of you, parallel to the ground. Step first with your right foot, then your left, then your right, then left, planting the tip of the pole in the box during the last two steps and using your forward momentum to swing by the pole (which is to your right) and into the pit. Have your coach watch you when you first try this. Don't raise your legs much; just

your knees up (C, D) and swing by the pole into the pit (E). You should land feet first, facing forward. Remember, for this exercise and the next, don't let go of the pole!

C   D   E

The Plant-and-Swing Drill with a Counterclockwise Half Turn

A

B

E

F

Everything in this drill is similar to the first, except for the addition of a counterclockwise half turn. If you're left-handed, your turn will be clockwise.

Make a six-step approach to the box, plant the pole (A), and with your coach's assistance (B), swing up and past the bar, lifting your knees as you do so (C, D). This time, however, as the pole reaches the vertical, make a counterclockwise half turn (E, F) and land on your feet (G), facing the direction you came from.

C

D

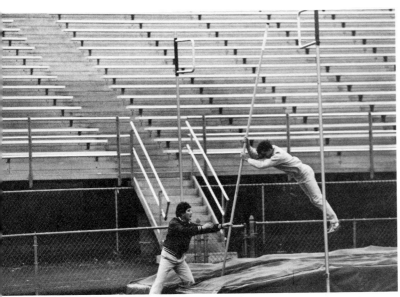

G

swing into the pit and get the feel of being lifted off the ground. Hang on to the pole. Don't let go of it! Now go back and start over, repeating this plant-and-swing drill 10 to 15 times, or until the sensation feels comfortable. Now you are ready for the next step in your training—all on the same day.

Hold the pole vertically in front of you and raise your right hand along it as high as you can. Now move your hand 12 to 15 inches higher than that point. To do that, of course, you'll have to pull the top of the pole toward you. Mark the new gripping point with a piece of tape. Find the left-hand gripping point (about shoulder width away from the right hand's), and mark that new point with tape also.

Step back four steps and repeat the drill, taking those four quick steps, left-right-left, planting the pole tip in the box, and swinging into the pit. As you plant the pole, keep a strong grip on it with your right hand, and a firm grip on it with your left. Do not let go of the pole as you swing into the pit. As you finish the vault, try to land standing, rather than falling on your seat. Repeat the drill 10 to 15 times. Then move back to a six-step approach and repeat the same drill, this time accelerating into the steps, then planting the pole and swinging up on it into the pit.

Your first day is not over yet! Now, using the six-step approach, swing up toward the pit—but as you do, make a half turn counterclockwise and land facing the direction you came from. Remember: hold on to the pole and remain standing when you land. Try this turning technique a number of times (shown on pages 46–47), until you begin to feel comfortable with it.

Okay. If you've had enough for one day, call it quits. Don't rush. However, if you still feel you have some vaults in you, place some high-jump standards up by the box and set a crossbar at, say, 5 feet. Keeping your grip at about 8 to 8½ feet, use the five-step approach to vault the bar. Make sure your coach is near the bar, to spot you and give advice. Five feet is going to seem like a relatively easy height to vault, but take your time and get the feeling of vaulting.

As soon as you clear the 5-foot bar, hang on to the pole, make that counterclockwise half turn, and land standing, facing the runway. Continue moving the bar up to heights of 6 feet, 6 feet 6 inches, 7 feet, 7 feet 6 inches, and 8 feet. This may take you a day, or it could take 3 or 4 days. No matter. Don't rush. Just vault, getting a feel for the pole and for a good takeoff over the bar.

Your coach can stand by the vault box and grab your pole as you start to take off, to help pull you into the actual vault. If you are right-handed, he should stand to the left of the box. Your coach can also stand about 5 feet in front and to the side of the box, and as you take off, give you a gentle push upward over the bar. Ultimately, though, you should learn to do as much vaulting as possible on your own, without having someone push you or pull you over the bar.

Do not be in a hurry to raise your grip during your first week of pole vaulting. You might want to move back to seven steps in your approach if you raise your grip to 9 or 10 feet, because you'll need more speed to get into the vault. Start off slowly in your approach, and increase your speed with each step. Keep your plant up high: on the plant, your right hand should be directly overhead, and you should have a good grip on the pole with both hands. Within a week or two, all of these techniques—the approach, plant, takeoff, turn, and landing—should be second nature to you. Once you have these down, you're ready to start work on the more advanced techniques of the pole vault.

TECHNIQUES OF THE VAULT

Most pole vaulters are right-handed, but those who are left-handed will have just as much success. The descriptions of the techniques that follow are for the right-handed vaulter. If you're a lefty, simply mirror the techniques to make them work for you—that is, think left for right and vice versa.

Whether you are left- or right-handed, understanding the basic techniques of the vault is the key to success. If you understand correct technique, you can eliminate many wrong turns and bad habits that would otherwise slow your progress—and worse, keep you from experiencing the success and fun that come from doing the event well.

The Pole Carry

Now that you're comfortable holding the pole at 9 or 10 feet, it's time to go for the most advanced carry. To start that carry properly, your right hand should be close to the top of a short (12- or 13-ft.) pole and your left hand below it, about shoulder width away. The distance between the hands should enable you to carry the pole comfortably on the approach, but not be so wide that it hinders the plant, takeoff, or rock-back phase of the vault (more on the rock-back later). Never grip the pole with your hands any closer than shoulder-width apart, or you will lose control going into the actual vault. For that matter, if your grip is too wide you will find it difficult to move into the rock-back position, which in turn will affect the outcome of the vault.

The precise hand grip is very important at the beginning, for it is difficult

50 to correct established faults as you develop. Place the pole tip on the ground, pointing toward the vault pit. With your right hand grip the end of the pole, curling only your thumb and the base of your index finger completely around it. The remaining three fingers of your right hand are held loosely, free from the pole, as the hand holds the pole at about waist level or slightly higher. At all times your right arm should remain relaxed and flexed. With your left hand at waist level, grip the pole, palm down and about shoulder distance from the right hand.

You will often see vaulters carrying the pole parallel to the ground at the very start of the run, with the tip out in front. I do not recommend that technique. Common as it is, it causes many problems for young vaulters in the run, the carry, and the acceleration toward the box:

1. The pole is heavy for the entire run (approach) and reduces the vaulter's acceleration speed toward the box.

2. Because the pole is heavy, it has a tendency to force the young vaulter into accelerating too early in the approach. Result: the vaulter decelerates near the end of the approach.

Gripping the Pole

(*Note:* The instructions here and at right apply to a right-handed pole vaulter. For you lefties out there, simply "mirror" the instructions; that is, think "left" when we say "right.") The right hand is the top hand, and it grips the pole chiefly with the thumb and the base of the index finger (A). The other three fingers are held loosely around the pole (B). The left hand grips the pole palm down, about shoulder width from the right hand (C).

A   B   C

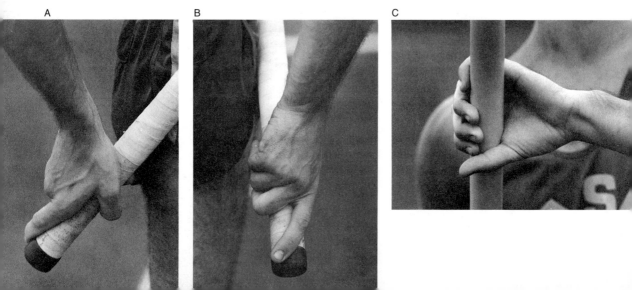

Carrying the Pole

A   B   C

The pole carry.
Start your carry by assuming the proper grip of the pole (A). With both arms flexed and elbows bent, lift the pole to a nearly vertical position in front of you (B). When the pole is in position, your left arm should be across your chest, your left elbow parallel to the ground, and your right hand at slightly below waist level (C). Keeping the pole tip up makes for a smoother, more comfortable approach start (D).

D

3. The awkwardness of this carrying method leads to awkward running form, poor body position, and awkward arm action.

How should you carry the pole?

After years of watching world-class vaulters, I am convinced that you should start with the pole held nearly vertical and close to your chest. By keeping the tip high and the center of mass of the pole just slightly in front of you, you will find that the pole feels lighter and easier to handle. Carry the pole with your left arm held across your chest and your right hand held at waist level. You'll discover that this position will help you feel comfortable during the entire initial portion of the approach and will help you maintain good running form for a longer period of time.

The Approach

The most important factor in the approach is successfully reaching the plant at the end of the run at a very fast speed, yet remaining in control of yourself and the pole.

Using check marks will help you develop a good step for the plant and

The approach.
The first five steps of your approach should be short, smooth, and slow (A, B). Try to increase your speed gradually (C), and avoid overstriding.

A

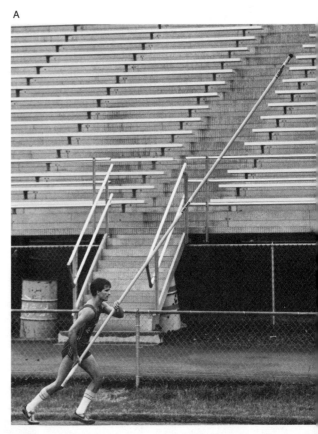

takeoff. There are three basic check marks that you should use, and each is equally important in developing a sound approach.

The first check mark is your starting point. If you're a beginner, this could be approximately 80 feet back from the box. For an intermediate vaulter who is vaulting at heights of 12 to 13 feet, this first mark might be about 100 feet back, and for the collegiate or world-class vaulter, it could be back as far as 120 to 140 feet. You'll have to experiment to find the starting point that is right for you. Once you've found it, measure the distance, and thereafter mark it off with adhesive or gaffer's tape or a shoe before any practice or competition. As your vaults improve, be prepared to lengthen the distance in order to increase your acceleration toward the box.

As you stand in preparation for your run, your right foot should be in back of your starting mark, the toes in line with the tape, and your left foot should be in line with the tape. Your right foot takes the first step of the run.

The second check mark should be six strides (16 to 18 feet) from the starting mark. This sixth-step checkpoint provides a useful reference point early in the run for gauging your stride and speed. If you overshoot or undershoot it by too great a margin, you will know that your stride is off and that you will

B   C

have to compensate to reach the proper takeoff point at the end of the run. Accelerate smoothly to the takeoff spot.

The third and last check mark is at the takeoff point, where your left foot makes the last step before you go into the actual pole plant. Like the sixth-step check mark, this mark helps you and your coach know whether your takeoff foot is too near or too far out for a sound takeoff.

Hints for a Good Approach. The speed of your approach will always determine the quality of your takeoff and the degree of bend in the vaulting pole. How fast should you run? As fast as you can, but in control. If you approach the takeoff with so much speed that you cannot control the last four steps in preparation for the vault, then you will find yourself slowing down—decelerating—rather than accelerating into the vault the way you'd like to. Beginning vaulters are especially prone to making this mistake.

Start your run slowly, and gradually increase your speed down the runway. This allows you to establish a good running rhythm without having to power out early in the approach. One of the biggest mistakes young vaulters make is starting their approach at a fast sprint. By starting too fast, the vaulter tends to reach top speed at the midpoint of the approach, and then, in his last two or three steps, because of either fatigue or overstriding, he finds himself slowing down going into the box for the plant. Overstriding is usually the bigger problem here. If the stride is too long in the last four steps or so, the vaulter will find himself planting the pole in the box too late, then stepping too far under the plant (more on this in a moment), and in the wrong takeoff position with not enough speed going into the takeoff.

Instead, those first five strides should be short, smooth, and slow. Think of yourself as a ball at the top of a hill, starting to roll down. Increase your speed gradually, smoothly, with as little effort as possible.

The Last Four Steps Into the Plant

No matter how long your approach, by the time you reach the last four strides going into the plant, you should have built up enough speed to be running as fast as you can, but at a controlled pace. During those last four strides, lower the pole so that it is at hip level and parallel to the ground. This pole-lowering phase should also be smooth and controlled—neither herky-jerky nor abrupt. If you do not lower it to hip level—that is, if the tip is still high and your top hand is below your waist—you will find yourself late in making the plant and unable to establish a good takeoff position as you shift your weight onto the pole.

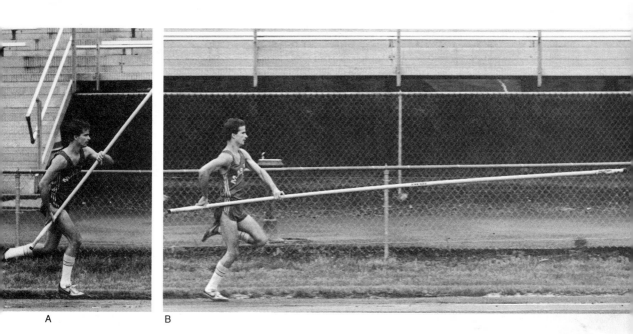

A   B

The last four steps into the plant.
As you near the end of your run, you should be running as fast as you can, but at a controlled pace, and you should begin lowering your pole (A). Four strides out from the last step, your pole should be parallel to the ground and level with your hip (B). You are now ready to make the transition leading to the pole plant.

The Transition Phase to the Plant

The transition phase to the plant is critical if the plant itself is to be efficient and accurate.

Again, moving the pole parallel to the ground during the last four steps, accelerate into the plant. Do not slow down. Do not maintain speed. Accelerate. Try to run into the plant as fast as you can. At this point you should be holding the pole steady, moving it neither forward nor backward, so that it is ready for its movement into the plant.

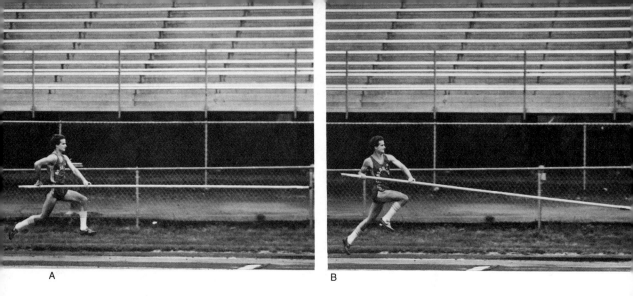

A   B

The transition phase to the plant.
With the pole parallel to the ground during the last four steps, accelerate into the plant (A, B). On the third step going into the takeoff, start the pole plant by keeping your left hand

Start the pole plant on the third step going into the takeoff. Your accumulated speed and the power of the pole as it bends take over on the last two steps before takeoff. Remember: the last step before takeoff should be with your left foot. To shift the pole from the parallel position and drop its tip into the box, keep your left hand and arm out in front and move your right hand up and out, in front of your forehead. Don't make the mistake of moving the pole forward first and then up and over your head, as this takes too long and will result in a late plant. Also avoid the improper technique called the "sidearm curl," in which the vaulter takes his right hand up by his ear and over his head. If you try it, you'll find that you always end up stepping too far under the pole and out of position for a good vault. Remember, move the pole up and out in front of your forehead, and reach as high as you possibly can. Run tall!

The Pole Plant

As you plant the pole in the box, your top (right) hand should be 1 to 3 inches above and in front of your forehead. The middle of your takeoff (left) foot

C   D

and arm out in front and moving your right hand up and out in front of your forehead (C). The last step before takeoff should be with the left foot (D), and the takeoff foot itself (the left one) should be in line with your top hand.

should be in line with your top hand. A good way of checking these positions is to see if the middle of your left foot is in line with your top hand when the pole is in the back of the box.

Your left arm guides the pole into the box and should be fairly straight at the moment of contact. The pole should be planted in line with your nose, not to the left or right. As the pole touches the box, let your left arm bend slightly, and move your elbow down and under the pole as you leave the ground. If you can keep your shoulders fairly square to the box at the plant, you will have a good chance of getting into a decent takeoff position after the plant. Whatever you do, do not let your left arm collapse completely. Keep it flexed but strong, and maintain pressure with it against the pole throughout the plant and takeoff.

Did you know that the plant should be completed before the takeoff foot has reached the ground? It's true, but it happens so fast that it's difficult to see this with the naked eye. Accept this concept, though: it will help you visualize a good body position as you move into the takeoff.

A   B   C

The pole plant.

As you plant the pole in the box, your right (top) hand should be 1 to 3 inches in front of your forehead, and the middle of your takeoff foot should be in line with your top hand. At the moment the pole makes contact with the box, your left arm should be fairly straight. The pole is planted in line with your nose, not to the left or right (A). As the pole touches the box, let your left arm bend slightly (B), and move your left elbow down and under the pole as you leave the ground (C). Keep your right arm extended. Try to keep your shoulders square to the box so that your body can get into a proper takeoff position after the plant.

Watching vaulters in action reminds us that there are many types of takeoffs; but there are a few common denominators among the successful ones. The takeoff should be an automatic reaction after the plant, and you can achieve this reflexive quality by doing lots of drill work during practice sessions or prior to a competition.

Going into the takeoff, your top hand should be directly over the takeoff foot. When leaving the ground, note if the left foot is too far under (that is, forward). Your initial takeoff action is similar to that for a long jumper. Drive forcefully off your left foot, driving your right knee forward and upward as you leave the ground. Keep your right arm as high as possible, keep your left arm in front of you, and work to keep the pole away from your body as much as possible. You will find that your left arm is now the stabilizing arm and will help you maintain control over both the pole and your body through the swinging movements. Whatever you do, do not bring your right knee up immediately. Do not try to get your body into a rock-back position early into the takeoff. This will cause you to stall out and fall short in the pit, and will eliminate any chance of getting into a good vertical position with the pole.

Remember: stay away from the pole, and use your left arm as a controlling lever throughout the takeoff and swing-through.

The takeoff.
Again, on the takeoff, your top hand should be directly over the takeoff foot and your right knee should drive forward and upward as you leave the ground. Your right arm is as high as possible, your left arm is in front of you, and the pole is away from your body (A). The left arm becomes the controlling lever on takeoff (B). Leap into the takeoff like a long jumper.

A

B

The Swing-Up and Rock-Back

An effective swing-up requires shortening the length of your body. On the takeoff, you are long and low to the pole. Now, however, as the pole begins its big bend, you have to get your body up to the top of the pole, and this requires you to shorten the length of the levers in your body by curling up and rocking back on the pole. Such a swing transfers your speed from the horizontal to the vertical. To make an effective swing-up, your left leg should leave the ground and be kept back and as straight as possible. Your right, or drive, knee should also stay pretty low and does not curl up until you are ready to shorten the body levers. Keep your left leg straight until it catches up with the right leg. Then curl both legs, which will move your body into the rock-back position, so

A

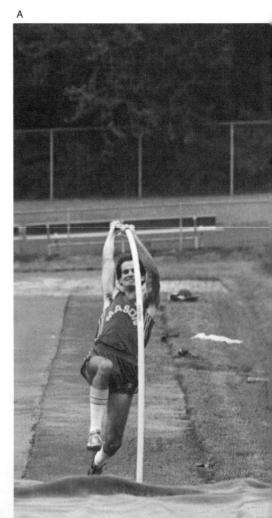

The swing-up and rock-back.
To perform a proper swing-up, your left leg, when leaving the ground, should be kept back and as straight as possible (A). The left leg stays back until it catches up with the right leg; then you curl both legs, which shortens the body's levers and moves you into the rock-back position (B, C).

named because you'll feel your body rocked backward—indeed, nearly upside down! As you go into the rock-back position, with your body tucked and both knees bent, do not pull with either arm, do not throw your head back, do not come out of the position too early, and do not look at the bar. Keep your eyes up, focusing close to your top hand or even higher, but avoid looking at the bar at all costs. Right now, you want to stay behind the pole and not let your hips drift out in front of it. By keeping your eyes on your top hand, you reduce the likelihood of hip drift. As you stay in the rock-back position, waiting for the pole to straighten, keep your left arm strong. The higher you are vaulting, the longer you must wait to come out of the rock-back position. Keep your left arm between your body and the pole, close to your chest.

B

C

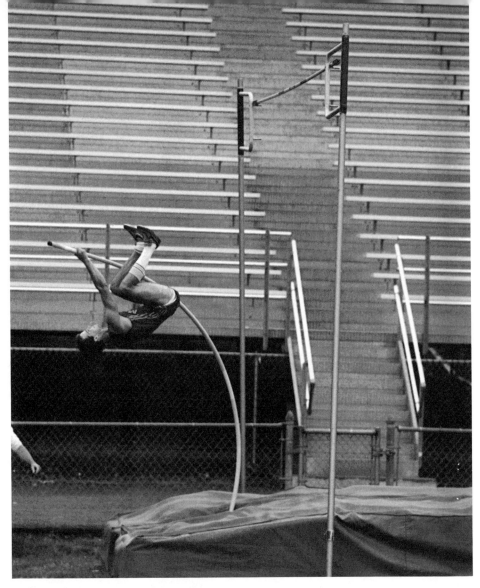

The rock-back position: another view.
The body is tucked, both knees are bent, the hips are behind the pole, and the left arm is strong. Remember, during this phase, keep your eyes on your top hand. That way, you reduce the chance of your hips drifting forward.

The Pull-Up, Turn, and Release

The pull-up begins when the pole comes back out of its bend. The keys to a good pull are (1) using your hips for movement and leverage, (2) keeping your body close to the pole, and (3) pulling (and a moment later, turning) quickly.

If your swing-up into the pole and your rock-back were good, you are now in a good position to pull on the pole. If your rock-back position was not good, you will have little if any pull on the pole because you'll find yourself trying to go over the bar on your side.

The pull and turn should begin when the pole is almost straight, and the two movements work almost together. Stay back on the pole and delay your pull as long as possible to gain the best possible vertical lift as the pole comes out of its bend. Think of pulling through your hips to move up the pole.

Your legs should move upward as they begin to straighten out from the rock-back position. Do not let your legs drift out and away from the pole. When your hips and center of gravity are at the height of the crossbar and the bottom of the pole is perpendicular, then pull and turn. Work to stay back on the pole as you are pulling and going into the turn. Remember, the pull and turn are very fast and powerful movements. At the end of the pulling phase, your arms are extended almost straight downward, the left arm reaches its full extension, releases, and then the right pushes up and releases.

The counterclockwise turn presents the left side and then the stomach (instead of the back) to the crossbar. In order to keep the center of gravity high as you go over the bar, keep your right leg up rather than turning and jackknifing the legs downward.

When the pole is absolutely straight, you should, in effect, be doing a handstand on it. As you lift away from the pole, your arms should be lifted away from the crossbar. Keep your thumbs rotated inward; this will help your elbows rotate away from the crossbar. Do not make the mistake of releasing the pole too early. Stay with the pole and use all of the energy stored in it.

You have made a good lift over the bar when you have pulled through the pole and made the turn with your right leg crossing over your left leg; your hips should be facing the ground but rising as you lift over the crossbar.

When clearing the bar, keep your thumbs turned in. Do not pull your arms back, or you will hit the bar with your chest. Move your arms out and up as you clear the bar. Let your lower legs (from the knees down) pull back. This action helps pull your chest back from the bar as you clear it.

As you fall toward the pit, be sure that you are safely clear of the vaulting box. Let yourself rotate slowly backward and land in the pit on your back, with your knees and feet in the air.

When adjusting the vaulting standards before your jump, keep them back toward the pit as far as you can. Do not adjust the standards toward the front of the vault box.

The Pull-Up, Turn, and Release

B

C

A

The pull-up and turn begin when the pole is almost straight. Move your hips and legs upward as they begin to straighten out from the rock-back position (A). When your hips and center of gravity are at the height of the crossbar and the pole is perpendicular to it, start your pull with both hands, and turn (B). At the end of the pull, the arms are extended almost straight down, the left arm reaches its full extension, and the left hand releases (C). Note, at that moment, how the right leg crosses behind the left as the body makes its counterclockwise half turn. The right arm pushes down on the pole, presenting the left side and stomach to the bar (D). Finally, the right hand releases as the lower legs pull back (E), the arms move out and up as you clear the bar (F), and your body rotates slowly backward so that you land in the pit on your back, with your knees and feet in the air (G).

D

E

F

G

Putting It All Together: The Pole Vault

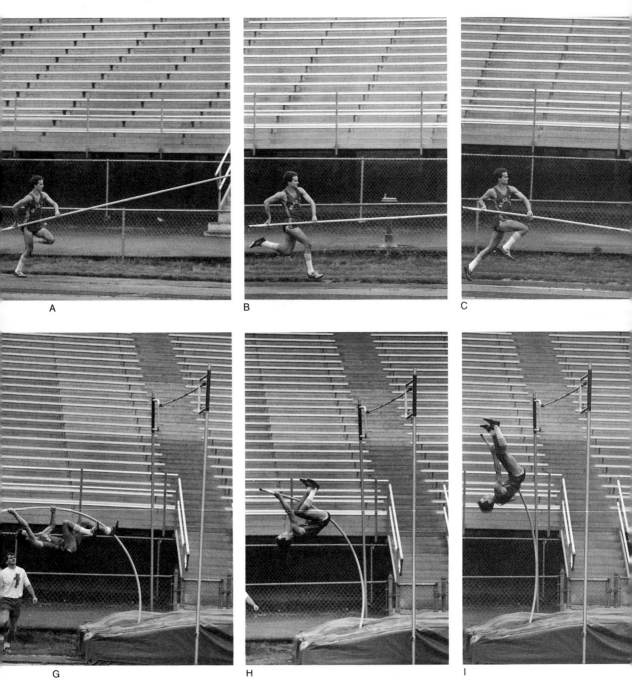

It's all here: from the last four steps before the plant (A, B, C), to the plant itself (D), the takeoff (E, F), the swing-up and rock-back (G, H), the pull-up (I), turn (J, K), release (L, M, N)…

D

E

F

J

K

L

(continued)

Putting It All Together: The Pole Vault (Cont.)

M   N   O

and, finally, the backward fall and landing (O, P, Q).

  Successful pole-vaulting requires a high degree of athletic ability and study to master its technique. Work with your coach, always vault with a spotter, and use the drills at the end of this chapter to help refine your technique.

P

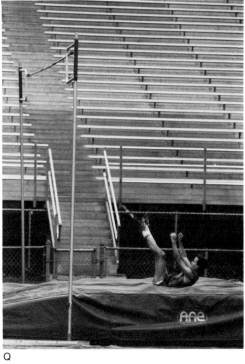

Q

COMMON PROBLEMS IN POLE VAULTING

Over the years, I have found that there are some common problems among all vaulters, whether beginners or experts. These problems can restrict your development if you do not correct them and can prevent you from attaining your best vaulting height.

Using too soft a pole. If you weight 150 pounds and you are using a pole that is rated at 130 pounds, you will find that that pole is too soft for you—it will prevent you from getting into a good rock-back position, it will feel "mushy" when it starts to straighten, and it will not give you good lift over the bar.

As a beginner, using too stiff a pole. If you weigh 140 pounds and you use a pole rated for 165 pounds, you will find it extremely difficult to bend the pole at takeoff. Without an adequate bend, you eliminate any chance for a good vault. Use a pole that is equal to your weight or 5 pounds lighter.

Using too long a pole. Vaulting poles range in length from 12 to 16 feet. If the grip of your top hand is comfortable at 13 feet, you should use a 13-foot pole, or at most a 14-footer. A longer, heavier pole is awkward to use and only impedes your progress while you are learning proper technique.

Gripping the pole too low. If you weigh 150 pounds and are using a grip of 13 feet 9 inches on a 14-foot pole rated for 150 pounds, chances are you are doing things pretty well. The length and rating of the pole are perfect for you, provided you can handle the grip. If, however, to handle the pole you have to choke up on it to, say, 12 feet, the pole's rating in effect changes to that for a person weighing 165 to 170 pounds. It will be too stiff for you to vault on. At the moment of takeoff, instead of having a nice round bend, the pole will have a very small bend or none at all. Without a good bend, a pole cannot store energy to be released at the top of the vault. Find a pole whose length and rating are right for you, and grip it at the end, as discussed earlier.

Failing to use a long enough approach run. We know that in order to gain top speed, we need to generate speed over a sufficient distance. I have found that many young vaulters use a (very short) run of 75 to 80 feet and therefore have a difficult time developing their top speed going into the plant. Sure, a beginner should use a somewhat abbreviated run because he is not vaulting great heights, but when you can vault up in the 12- to 14-foot range, your run should be longer—from 100 to 120 feet, or more if you can handle it. By using a longer approach, you can start slowly and accelerate smoothly over a longer time, allowing you to be at top speed during the last four steps into the plant.

Slowing down at the plant. Keep your speed up and think about attacking the plant and takeoff. Start your approach slowly, and increase your speed all the way through the approach.

Planting the pole too late. Keep your pole carry high going into the plant. If your right hand is below your waist, you will have to move it a long distance to get to a fully extended position over your head. This takes time, and it will often cause you to plant the pole too late. Keep your top hand above your hip, thereby reducing the distance your hand has to travel and giving you a faster plant.

Not getting a high plant on takeoff. When you plant the vaulting pole, your right hand should be high above your forehead and your right arm extended to its maximum. This will give you a good high plant. If you do not extend your top (right) arm fully, the plant will be too low, and the time and area in which you can take off and swing up onto the pole will be drastically reduced. You will also find that the pole will feel stiff and difficult to bend on takeoff.

Driving the right knee upward too early in the takeoff. As you take off after the pole plant, your right knee should move forward and upward slightly. Do not bring the knee up too quickly into the takeoff, or you will stall out over the bar. Drive your right knee forward and upward as long as you can throughout the takeoff so that the pole gets a proper deep bend in it. How high should you drive your knee? If it is even with or higher than the level of your hips, it is too high. Drive your knee no higher than just below hip level.

Going into the rock-back position too early. You will find that as you first learn to vault, you will want to get into a rock-back position very quickly. Resist that impulse and do just the opposite. Delay the rock by keeping your left leg back. Let your lower arm remain strong (don't collapse it too early), and allow the pole to bend and store energy while you are still in a hanging position.

Letting your lower arm collapse as you move into the takeoff. If you let your arm collapse, you will find that you are in a rock-back position too early. Keep pushing with the left (lower) arm, and allow your hips to stay behind the pole. Collapsing your lower arm on takeoff can also cause your hips to drift out in front of you, making you stall out over the bar or strike the bar on your way up.

Stalling out. Stalling out means that instead of rising up over the bar, you either come down on it, land shallow in the pit (near the vaulting box), or worse, fall back onto the runway. It's often caused by throwing your head back in order to get your hips up on the rock-back, and by keeping your left arm too stiff and strong during that phase. Instead, let your left arm form a right angle, which in turn will allow your hips to come back into the rock-back without your having to jerk your head back.

You can also stall out by rocking up on the pole too early. Stay at the bottom and let your pole move forward into the pit.

SELECTING THE PROPER POLE

You and your coach should be very careful in selecting the proper pole for your vaulting. Trying to vault with the wrong-size pole is like trying to play golf with only a putter, or trying to play tennis with a Ping Pong paddle—you might be able to do it, but your performance would be severely hampered.

How do you go about selecting the proper pole? Start by noting your weight and your best vaulting height. Let's say that you weigh 120 pounds and you've never vaulted before. Given the latter fact, you should start with the shortest allowable pole, which is 12 feet, and choose one rated for 120 pounds. Look for the pole rating along its shaft. Most manufacturers would list a 12-foot pole rated for 120 pounds as a 12020.

If you are an intermediate jumper, you should weigh these variables in choosing a pole:

- Your weight. (Let's say it's 150 pounds.)
- Your best vault. (Let's say it's 13 feet 6 inches.)
- The length of your current pole. (Let's say it's 13 feet.)
- Where you grip that pole. (Let's say at 12 feet 6 inches.)
- The quality of your vaulting technique at takeoff. (Let's say it's okay.)

With these factors in mind, I would suggest two poles for consideration:

1. a 14-foot pole rated for 155 pounds (14055 medium flex), or
2. a 15-foot pole rated for 145 pounds (15045 soft flex).

Why these two? Mainly because they'll allow you to move your hand grip up another 6 to 15 inches from its position on your current pole, and both will give you more power for higher vaults. They may feel a little stiff at first, but as you continue to practice, you'll make the adjustments and find that you can handle either pole nicely. Further, you'll still be within a very safe vaulting range in terms of both your weight and the strength of the pole. Because the shorter recommended pole is rated at 155 pounds (a heavier rating than your weight), it will give you a strong bend and great uncoiling power as you start to come out of the vault. The longer pole will allow you an even higher grip, but is still soft enough to handle your weight.

If you do not change the height of your grip, moving up to a longer pole means moving into a stiffer one as well. This is an important point for all vaulters and coaches to understand. If you raise your grip just 5 inches, you actually reduce the same pole's stiffness by about 5 pounds. For example, let's say you move from a 13-foot 6-inch pole to a 14-foot pole with a rated weight of 150 pounds, but your top grip remains at 13 feet 6 inches. The pole will feel stiff to you. However, if you raise your top grip 5 inches (to 13 feet 11 inches), the pole will feel softer because you have increased the distance from the center of the pole (bending point) to the ends, thus giving you a bigger bend and a softer-feeling pole. The pole will feel and act like one rated for 145 pounds.

And if you lowered your hand from 13 feet 6 inches to 13 feet? The pole would feel very stiff and would actually give you the sensation of a pole rated for 155 pounds.

When should you move to a longer pole? If you are repeatedly bending your pole beyond a 90-degree angle, it's time to change poles. When you and your coach feel that you have used your current pole to its maximum (based on the grip that you have on the pole and the height you are vaulting), try moving to a pole that is 6 to 12 inches longer but rated at about the same weight. Raise your grip on this pole 3 to 4 inches above your previous grip, and you'll find that the adjustment is pretty easy. What's more, you'll start to vault higher because of the higher grip. By going to a longer pole, you can raise your center of gravity (hips) higher at the moment of release than you can with a shorter pole.

Always try to start using a stiff pole as soon as your speed and technique allow you. Remember, the stiffer the pole, the higher you can vault—provided your speed and technique are developing. Never change poles simply for the sake of change. Change poles when yours appears to be too soft and fails to give you good lift over the bar. Never make a drastic change, such as going from a 14-foot, 150-pound-test pole to a 14-foot, 165-pound-test. Make pole weight changes at 5- to 10-pound increments at most, and length changes at 6- to 12-inch increments.

DRILLS FOR THE VAULTER

There are many drills that can help you, and every coach and athlete has his or her favorite. What's important is understanding a drill's purpose—what performing it can accomplish for you as a vaulter.

Approach Drills

Sprints. On a running track, sprint 30 to 50 meters, using good acceleration and going full speed over the last 10 meters of the run. Repeat this drill 5 times, with at least a 2-minute rest between sprints. Do these sprints two to three times per week.

Plyometric Drills. Plyometric drills can easily aid the development of a vaulter's leg strength and leg speed. See the horizontal jumping drills described in Chapter 2.

Sprinting with the Pole. If you're a beginner, hold the vaulting pole so that it is perfectly balanced in your hands. If you are using a 14-foot pole, place your top hand about 8 feet up from the bottom, your bottom hand 6 feet up. This should balance the pole in your hands and allows you to develop good sprinting posture as you train. Sprint for 30 to 50 meters, accelerating to full speed over the last 10 meters of each run. Rest 2 to 3 minutes between runs. Run 5 to 10 sprints at least three times a week in the early part of the season, and then reduce this to twice per week during the competitive season.

As the season progresses, raise your grip higher on the pole, so that at the end of the season you are running with the pole just as if you were competing.

Sprinting with a Weighted Bar. Use a pipe or bar that is short but gives you some weight (4 to 5 pounds) in your hands. This drill should be done in the early part of the season, and you should run at about 75 percent speed. Work on body posture and arm carriage. Run 20 to 30 meters, rest for 30 seconds, and repeat. Do this 10 times, at least three times a week.

Downhill Sprints. These are great for developing speed. Run with your team's sprinters or jumpers if you can. The hill should be a gradual incline (4 to 6 degrees), not a steep slope. Accelerate smoothly down the hill and run for 40 to 60 meters. Rest 2 minutes between runs, and repeat 10 to 12 times. Do this twice a week.

Running Long Jumps. Without a pole, take 10 to 15 short approaches (that is, from a distance of about 40 feet), and jump into the pit like a long jumper, landing on your feet. This drill provides great practice for takeoffs and body positions.

Plant Drills

Plants Against the Wall. In the gym or outside the field house, use a wall to practice your plant. Take three steps going into the plant, place the pole tip at the base of the wall, and plant the pole as you drive up and obtain a slight bend in the pole. Do this exercise 10 to 20 times daily.

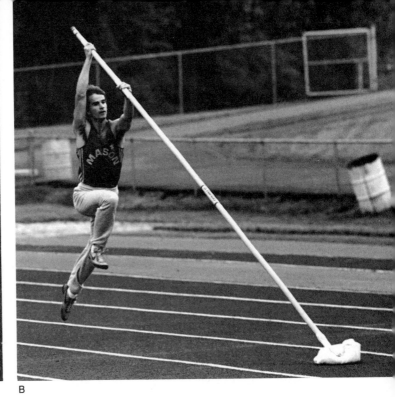

A   B

The towel drill.
Using a towel to simulate a vault box (A), practice full-speed plants on the track (B) without vaulting in order to fine-tune your strides and improve your acceleration into the plant.

Plants Into the Box, Using a Three- to Five-Step Approach. Walk into the plant using a three-step approach, plant the pole, and get a small bend in it. Now back up to a five-step approach and accelerate slightly into the plant on the last two strides. Get a bigger bend in the pole but stay in control. Rebound back slightly as the pole straightens, and hang on to the pole.

Towel Drill. Carrying the pole, practice your full run on the track using a towel as a simulated plant box, and plant (but don't vault) at full speed. This is a good drill for checking your strides and for developing acceleration into the plant. Do this twice a week, 8 to 10 times per session.

Jump-Plant Drill. Hold your pole 12 to 18 inches above your head. Take four accelerating steps. Jump off your left foot and plant the pole explosively onto the runway or grass infield. Swing through. Do not rock up. Hang, and fall forward, landing on your feet. Repeat 10 to 12 times.

Takeoff Drills

Six- to Eight-Step Approach, Plant, and Swing-Through. Accelerate into the plant, take off, and swing up onto the pole, landing on your buttocks or back in the pit. Repeat 5 to 10 times. Start with your grip low and move up into your regular grip as you progress through the drill. This is a good warm-up every day and for every meet.

Short Approach, Low Vault, Using a Light Pole. Take a 9- to 11-step approach and keep the bar low (at least 2 feet below your regular vaulting height). Work with a light pole rated below your weight, remembering to go easy into the approach, not at full speed. This is a technical drill, great for relaxation, fun, and confidence. Work on it once a week for the entire practice season.

Takeoff and Swing-Through Using the Spirit Trainer or a Lightweight Pole. The specially made training pole by UCS Spirit is designed for practicing plants and takeoffs. It is a soft pole with great strength, but it will not lift you over the bar. (You can get a similar flexion out of a lightweight pole, but you must exercise great caution and not use a pole rated more than 20 pounds below your weight.) Take 20 to 25 plants and swing-throughs. This is a great drill for improving technique early in the season.

Takeoff and Swing-Through to the Back of the Pit, Landing on Your Buttocks. Plant the pole in the box, keep your left arm strong, and land in the back of the pit. This exercise helps improve body control and prevents your left arm from collapsing too soon. Perform this drill 3 to 4 times, and use it as a preliminary warm-up for meets or practice.

Rope Drills in the Gym. Using a gymnastic rope suspended from the gym ceiling, run and grab the rope as you take off, and work on a proper swing-through. Another good drill is to have your coach swing the rope slightly toward you as you approach, so that you can grab it on the upswing. Hang momentarily, rock back, and then turn over on the rope just as you would on the vaulting pole. When the rope swings back to the point where you first grabbed it, you can lower your feet, hop off, and keep running in the same direction in which you began.

COACHING TIPS
FOR THE POLE VAULT

• Have the vaulter establish a good run and approach, using 18 to 22 strides.

• Observe the way the vaulter holds the pole during the initial phase of the approach run. It should be nearly vertical.

• Does the vaulter slowly lower the pole as he approaches the vaulting pit? He should use the pole to help accelerate into the plant.

• Stand in the coach's box and observe where the vaulter plants his takeoff foot. Is he hitting his mark correctly? Check for deceleration during the last four strides.

• Four steps away from the plant, the vaulting pole should be parallel to the ground, with the top hand close to and slightly above the hip.

• The vaulter should start the plant three strides out. He should be quick and aggressive.

• The pole should move up and forward during the plant. The vaulter's top hand should be at full extension above his head and slightly in front of his forehead.

• Check the vaulter's takeoff foot. If you could draw a line from the vaulter's top hand to the ground, the takeoff foot should be just touching it.

• On takeoff, the vaulter's free knee should drive up and toward the pole.

• The takeoff foot and leg should remain back. Have the vaulter try to get that "hanging" feeling. He shouldn't rock back too early.

• Remind the vaulter to keep slight pressure on the lower arm at takeoff.

• On the rock-back, do the vaulter's knees flex and retract toward the body? Does he try to keep his body close to the pole? His hips should not drift out in front of the pole. They should stay behind it.

• The vaulter should not be looking for the bar. Instead, he should keep his eyes focused on his top hand. Doing so can help him keep his body in proper alignment with the pole.

• Watch the vaulter's pull-up. He should initiate it when his hips are above the level of his shoulders, and he should lift *up!*

• Keep the standards (the two braces that hold the bar) back as far as possible into the pit so that the vaulter has vertical space to clear the bar.

• The vaulter should land squarely on his back in the middle of the pit, well back from the vaulting box.

SAMPLE TRAINING WEEKS FOR THE POLE VAULT

The sample one-week workouts here are intended to give you and your coach an opportunity to see how varied a workout can be during the training seasons. Many vaulters may have the opportunity to vault indoors during the indoor track season. Others may have no vaulting season indoors, and simply have an outdoor season. Review the workouts, noting their variety, and determine which might work best for you.

The Off-Season (October–February)

Monday

Warm-up: 20 min. Include easy jog followed by stretching.
Rope climbs: 20 feet, 4–6 times.
Pull-ups on the high bar: 8–10 times, 3 sets.
Dips on the parallel bar: 8–10 times, 3 sets.
Hip flexion drill.
Backward roll vault to a handstand: 5–6 times, 3 sets.
Arch push-ups between two boxes.
Wall push-ups: toes on a wall, facing toward a wall, and about 18 inches from the wall. Do 20 to 50 per set, depending on your physical condition.
Warm-down: jog 1–2 miles.
Plyometrics.

Tuesday

Warm-up: 20 min.
Stride: 200 meters for form running, 3 times.
Run with short pole: 30–40 meters, 8–10 times.
Plant drills: in front of mirror if possible, 10 min.
Work with weights:

Exercises	Sets	Reps
Incline presses	3–5	3–6
Half squats	3–5	6–12
Back hyperextensions	3	15–20
Stomach crunch sit-ups	3–5	20–25
Leg curls	2	10–12
Leg extensions	2	10–12
Pullovers	1	8–12

Warm-up: 20 min.
Stride: 100 meters for form running, 5 times.
Plant drills: against wall or vault box, 15–25 times.
Rope climbing: 15-foot rope, 5 times.
   Hand over hand without legs
   Hand over hand without legs at a 90° angle
   Upside down (hook fist and legs around the rope)
   Upside down push-ups (left hand below the right)
Handwalking: 10–12 feet, 5 times.
Parallel bar work: 20 min.
   Dips
   Dips with legs at a 90° angle
   Pull-twist drills
Jog 1–2 miles.
Plyometrics.

Thursday

Jog and warmup: 30–35 min.
Stretching exercises: 20 min.
Pole carry and imitation plants, 15–20 times.
Pole runs, plant into a towel, in the gym: 20–25 min.
Light warm-down: 10–12 min.

Friday

Warm-up: 20 min.
Weight work: 60 min. (follow Tuesday schedule).
Jog 2 miles.

Pre-Season (March)

Monday

Warm-up: 20 min. Get lots of stretching in today.
50-meter sprints for acceleration: 3 times.
50-meter runs with the pole: 3 times.
Pole plants, and swing-through drills into the pit: 30 min.
Light bounding: 50 meters, 5–8 times.
Jog 800 meters. Stretch and cool-down.

Tuesday

Warm-up: 20 min.
Pole vault drills, working on the plant: 15 min.
Weight work. 45–50 min.
Cool-down: 20 min.

Wednesday

Warm-up: 20 min.
Film analysis of pole vaulters with coach.
Duplicate some movements that were observed in the films: 30 min.
   Approach runs
   Pole plants
   Rock-backs or swing-throughs
Cool-down: 20 min.

Thursday

Warm-up: 20 min.
Short run and low grip drill with the pole: 20 times.
   Approach
   Plant
   Swing-throughs
Upper body plyometric drills: 30 min.
Bounding and box drills: 20 min.
Cool-down: 10–12 min.

Friday

Warm-up: 20 min.
Work with vaults over a bar using short runs and low grip: 60 min.
Weight work: 45–50 min.
Cool-down: 20 min.

Competitive Season (April–June)

Monday

Warm-up: 20 min.
Short run and low grip drills with the pole: 60 min.
Sprint drills: 30-meter acceleration sprints, 5 times.

Bounding: 15 min.
Cool-down: 10–12 min.

Tuesday

Warm-up: 20 min.
Drills for the plant and takeoff: 40 min.
Weight work: 45 min.
Cool-down: 10–12 min.

Wednesday

Warm-up: 20 min.
Short run and plants: 10 min.
Progressive vaults for height: low 2 times, medium 3 times, high 4 times.
High vaults above lifetime best: 5 times.
Upper-body plyometrics: 20 min.
Cool-down: 10–12 min.

Thursday

Warm-up: 20 min.
200-meter sprints with acceleration at the end: 5 times.
Weight work: 45–50 min.
Cool-down: 10–12 min.

Friday

Review track films of the vault and of your own vaulting.
Warm-up and stretching: 30 min.
Jog 2 miles.

Saturday

Competition day: Start your vaults at a low height and work your way up.

4

The High Jump

Unlike the pole vault, the high jump is an event in which you can excel rather quickly, *if* you learn the basics and then take the time to build upon them. For years coaches—myself included—thought that body height was the most important physical attribute for becoming a good jumper. Now we know that speed, quickness, and agility are equally important, and that an athlete can overcome a height disadvantage and become a good jumper if he or she can develop these other attributes.

THE EVOLUTION OF THE HIGH JUMP

For years high jumpers competed in the event by performing a technique called the Straddle. For a left-footed takeoff, the jumper would approach the bar from the left at a shallow angle, using an eight-step run, and on the eighth step hurl his body—right leg and arm first—over the bar. His stomach would be facing the bar as he cleared it, and he would roll and land on his back. It worked fine, but it appeared that unless a superhuman jumper came along, the Straddle would limit the world high-jump record to slightly over 7 feet. Indeed, when the famous Russian high jumper Valery Brumel jumped 7 feet 1.75 inches at the Olympics in Tokyo, it seemed nothing short of miraculous.

Then in 1968 along came a lanky young American named Dick Fosbury, who revolutionized the high jump by taking a curved approach to the bar and crossing it head first, on his back. He looked as if he were just flopping into the landing pit, and the sporting press quickly dubbed this new technique the Fosbury Flop.

At the 1968 Olympics in Mexico City, American Dick Fosbury unveiled a revolutionary high-jump technique now known as the Flop. Result: a gold medal for Fosbury and exciting new possibilities for high jumping thereafter.

Did it improve the record heights in the high jump? You bet. Fosbury himself won a gold at the 1968 Olympics in Mexico City, clearing the bar at 7 feet 4.25 inches—a height undreamt of only a few years before. Since then, jumpers using the Flop have gone on to clear heights greater than 7 feet 11 inches, and the likelihood of pushing the height envelope further remains strong. (At this writing, the world record is 8 feet.)

Why does the Flop work so well? In a word, because it's efficient. It allows the jumper to convert linear motion accrued during the approach into vertical (jumping) motion far more efficiently than the Straddle ever could. Rather than trying to elevate the legs first as in the Straddle, the Flop starts by elevating the head and upper body, which are closer to the bar to begin with. The Flop is Dick Fosbury's legacy to the high jump—and the track-and-field world is grateful he invented it.

A

Getting started in the high jump: Jumping without a bar. From a few feet off to one side of the high jump, and without the bar in place, run toward the pit and jump, taking off from one foot (A) and trying to land on your seat (B, C).

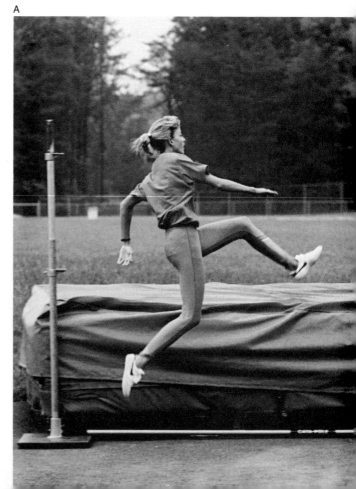

GETTING STARTED IN THE HIGH JUMP

If you've never high-jumped before, the best way to learn the event is through the following progression:

First, make sure you practice all the maneuvers below with a modern foam rubber landing pit. A full foam pit measures 16 feet 4 inches by 13 feet 1½ inches and is 22 to 26 inches thick. It is *absolutely* required for doing the Flop.

Now, without the bar in place, position yourself a few feet off to one side of the high jump, run toward it, and leap into the pit. Try to take off from one foot, not two, and land sitting in the pit, not on your back or stomach. Note how you have to turn your body in order to land in the sitting position. Note also which foot feels more natural and comfortable to take off from. Generally, right-handed jumpers take off from their left foot, on the right side of the pit.

B
C

The Scissors Jump

Once you've practiced without a bar for a while, set the bar at about the same level as the high-jump pit and stand back at an angle, about 25 feet from it. Run toward the bar, taking off for the jump with your outside leg, and scissoring over the bar with your inside leg. To scissor, simply raise your inside leg over the bar as you jump off the outside leg.

If you are right-handed, you will probably want to start on the right-hand side of the pit as you face it. Your takeoff foot is your left foot, and your scissoring leg over the bar will be your right leg. As you near the takeoff, swing both arms back, then powerfully lift them to shoulder height as you plant your takeoff foot. Your inside (right) leg comes up and drops over the bar, and your

The scissors jump.
With the bar set at a low height, start a few steps back from the right side of it (if you are right-handed) and make your approach (A). As you near the bar, swing your arms back (B), then powerfully lift them to shoulder height as you take off on your left foot (C). Your inside

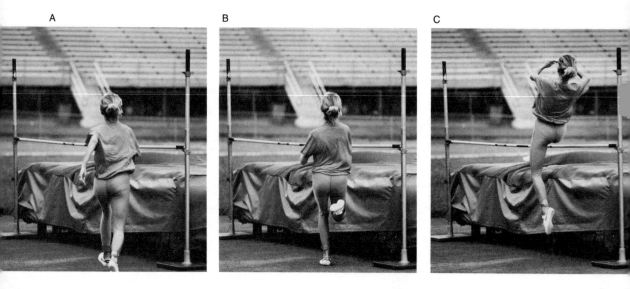

A   B   C

left leg scissors up and over it as if you were hopping a fence in a sitting position. If you perform this jump properly, you should land on your right hip. The Scissors is lots of fun, and it helps you develop a good approach angle as you start to learn the Flop.

Once you feel comfortable doing the Scissors, move a few steps farther back and try to establish an appropriate starting point for your approach to the bar. Work on a five-step approach. If you come in from the right side, your first and last step should be with your left foot. Take five steps, plant your takeoff foot so that it points to the inside of the far high-jump standard, and scissor-jump over the bar. Once you've found a good starting point for the five-step approach, mark it on the jumping apron. You are now starting to develop your approach step.

(right) leg comes up and drops over the bar (D), and your left leg scissors over after it (E). Try to land on your right hip.

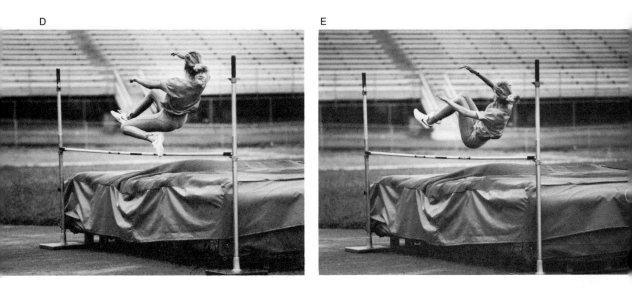

D   E

The Flop

Dick Fosbury transformed the basic Scissors jump into the Flop by presenting his back to the bar and going over head and shoulders first. In order to move to this next, critical step in high jumping, work first without the bar, taking your five-step approach and planting with your left foot (if you are coming from the right side). This time, however, turn your body slightly to the left as you leave the ground, jump with your shoulders first, then your back, and land in the middle of the pit on your back. Here, especially, you can see why a good cushiony landing pit is essential. A Flopper lands on the whole back, from the shoulders to just above the buttocks. Practicing without a proper landing pit is an invitation to serious injury. *Don't do it!*

In both the Scissors and the Flop, a powerful double-arm lift at the moment of takeoff helps convert forward momentum into upward velocity. After you've tried the Flop a number of times without the bar, put the bar in place (at pit level again), and perform the jump over it. Remember: (1) five-step approach; (2) as you near the takeoff, swing your arms back; (3) plant your left foot and forcefully raise your arms to shoulder height; (4) turn your body slightly to the left as you leave the ground; (5) clear the bar with your head and shoulders first, then your back; (6) land on your back in the middle of the pit. That's all you need to know to get started in the high jump. To progress, however, takes concentration and effort.

CORRECT TECHNIQUE FOR THE HIGH JUMP

Once you feel comfortable going over the bar at lower heights, it's time to start refining your technique through every phase of the high jump, setting the bar at progressively challenging heights. A good high jump—one where you clear the bar without dislodging it from its pegs—can be divided into seven parts, or phases: (1) the approach, (2) the curve, (3) the plant position, (4) the takeoff, (5) the jump, (6) the bar clearance, (7) the landing. The quality of your technique in each phase can spell the difference between a successful and an unsuccessful jump, so it's important to master each phase through systematic practice and self-visualization.

For now, let's look carefully at those seven phases.

Phase One: The Approach

The key to a good approach is consistency, which includes being able to get off a good jump every time you approach the bar. This means being at the speed and position you want in order to achieve a good takeoff every time. By being consistent in your approach, you'll be able to jump higher, longer, and more successfully.

The purpose of the approach is to get you to the takeoff point and in a good position so that, at a precise moment, you can get a powerful takeoff. When you began learning to high jump, you practiced a simple five-step approach. Now it's time to lengthen the approach and redefine the path it follows. High jumpers make part of their approach to the bar in a curved, or arcing, path, and the entire approach involves three aspects:

1. the length of the run (a minimum of nine strides),
2. the degree of curvature of the arc as you approach the bar, and
3. the speed of the run through the arc and into the foot plant.

When it is diagrammed, a good approach run looks a bit like the letter J. The first part of the approach should be a straight line for four to six strides. If you make your approach from the right side of the bar (which means that your takeoff foot for the actual jump is your left foot), you should start your stride count by stepping off with your left foot. Let's walk through this approach.

1. Start your approach about 12 feet out from the inside, or near, standard and about 40 to 50 feet back.

2. From a standing position with your left foot back, start your approach by stepping forward with your left foot.

3. Take four accelerating strides. The fourth step will be on your right foot.

4. From the fourth step (right foot), begin curving to the left—as if you were starting a quarter-turn on a circle.

5. Take five running steps, continuing to accelerate into the arc.

6. Your ninth step will be with your left foot, which is your takeoff foot. The takeoff point should be in line with the near (right) standard of the high-jump bar. Try to get your heel in line with the standard.

It's possible to have an approach run of 11 to 13 strides to the bar; some world-class high jumpers use as many as 15 to 17 strides. However, when starting out, work on body control and on developing a good approach, and do not increase the length of your approach run until you know that you need more speed for your jump, or more time and distance to get into a good running form leading up to the arc turn and foot plant. It's important to understand that the speed of your approach in the high jump must be controlled, and that running as fast as you can at the bar isn't necessary. Learn what your basic and maximum control speeds are. Do not compare yourself to other jumpers. Be your own jumper.

Your first step in the entire approach is one of the most important, as it sets up the entire run. If you don't make the first step in the same, consistent manner every time, the rest of the approach will always be faulty. If your first step varies, it means that you are pushing off with different degrees of force each time, and if that's the case, each of the other eight to ten strides will be off, and you'll be forced to make some type of adjustment as you approach the bar.

As you near the fourth step, your body should be balanced with a very slight forward lean, and you should be accelerating. Do not lean too far forward, or your hips will be in a poor position entering the takeoff, which in turn will affect your foot position as it makes the plant.

Phase Two: The Arc, or Curve

Now the question is, how long should the arc be? Where should you initiate it?

The size of the arc will vary from jumper to jumper, and depends on the jumper's height and limb length. As a general rule, an arc radius of 13 to 15 feet is comfortable and effective for most jumpers. However, this radius can range up to 15 to 18 feet, depending upon how tall you are and how well you can run the arc. If you are somewhat slow, you might want to run an arc that is only 13 feet in radius. If you are strong and fast, you might choose a radius from 15 to 17 feet. Smoothness and control are the keys to running a good arc.

Always place a "turn mark" on the approach surface during your practice sessions. The turn mark is that point where you will start your five-step arc. Always hit the turn mark with your outside foot. Do not hit the mark on your takeoff foot. Such a mark will help you learn when to enter the curve and change your degree of lean. Good leaning position (into the circle and away from the bar) is important because it translates into a strong jump effort after the plant. As you go into the turn, do not make a great effort to run faster; think instead about maintaining speed. Yes, some mental and physical acceleration is recommended, but overall you should approach the last three strides under control and with good speed.

Whatever you do, do not slow down, for that will cause you to take too long a last stride and put you into a poor takeoff position after the plant. Instead, run *into* the plant position, and concentrate most on smoothly executing the last three steps.

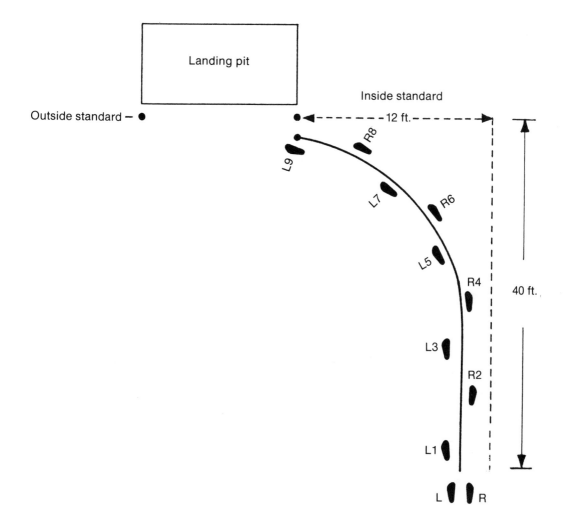

Landing pit

Outside standard — ●

Inside standard

●◄ — — — — — — — 12 ft. — — — — — — ►

R8

L9

L7

R6

L5

R4

40 ft.

L3

R2

L1

L R

The approach.

This diagram illustrates a nine-step approach. Note that the beginning jumper starts at a point 12 feet to the right of the crossbar (more advanced jumpers start at a point 16 feet to the right), and about 40 feet back (the precise distance back depends on a jumper's speed and stride length). After the fourth step, the jumper begins the arc phase of his five-step arc approach. To find the starting point and arc size that work for you, you must experiment with your coach, always using only five steps in the arc phase itself.

Phase Three: The Plant Position

The length of your last step depends upon your style of jumping. If you are a power jumper, driving almost straight up and over the bar, make a long last step into the plant. If you are a speed jumper, taking off a little farther out from the bar and landing deep into the pit, your last step will be slightly shorter. Your jumping technique dictates your foot plant. In either case, the plant should be made so that your foot is pointing toward the far standard. Do not plant your foot parallel to the crossbar. If you do, you'll find that executing a good back layout as you go over the bar will be extremely difficult. Planting your foot parallel to the bar can also put you in a poor takeoff position. Remember, keep your foot pointed toward the inside of the far standard.

D

C

Plant Position for the Speed Jumper. As you near the moment when you plant your takeoff foot, the next-to-last stride, no matter what your jumping style, is a key reference point. If you are a speed jumper, this penultimate stride should be slightly longer than your previous strides. Why? Because it will help you lower your center of gravity in preparation for the last stride, which is meant to start lifting you over the bar. Try to bound or drive into the penultimate stride so that you lower your body position. Think of letting the ground come up to meet your foot. For a left-footed takeoff, your right leg takes the penultimate step.

If you've done a good job in lowering your body and taking a long penultimate stride, the last stride (with your left foot) will be shorter and you'll be on the rise coming off the plant foot. This approach and plant are key components to a style of jumping known as the "speed flop"—a style that has been used successfully by many jumpers.

Plant position for the speed jumper.
If you are a speed jumper, your penultimate step should be slightly longer than the previous strides (A). This lowers your center of gravity in preparation for the last stride and is meant to start lifting you as you go into that last step (B, C, D). Always plant your takeoff foot so that your heel is in line with the near standard.

B   A

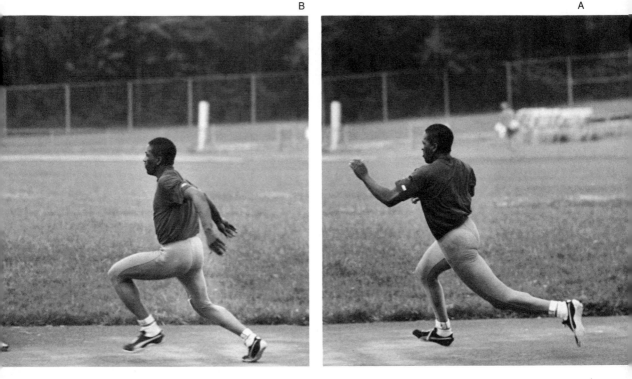

Plant Position for the Power Jumper. Another popular variation of the basic Fosbury Flop is the Power Flop, which is characterized by a shorter penultimate step and a longer last step. Let's say you take your penultimate step with your right foot. Work on getting your arms back and deep behind you as you take that step. This will help shorten the penultimate stride, which in turn will (1) lengthen your last stride, (2) lower your center of gravity, and (3) allow you to drive powerfully straight up and over the bar. Place your plant foot about 2 to 3 feet from the near standard and crossbar.

Your arms, which have moved in a normal running position up to the penultimate stride, play a big role in the takeoff for the Power Flop. As you make your plant (here, with the left foot), your arms, flexed at the elbow, should drive upward, close to your hips, to head level. The drive should be quick and powerful. As you plant, your body should be leaning away from the bar at about a 15- to 20-degree angle, but at the moment just before takeoff, your body should be vertical. You might want to think of this as the "loading position."

E

D

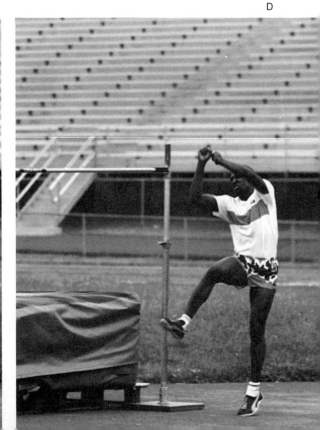

Phase Four: The Takeoff

What you do with your arms on the takeoff will greatly determine how high you jump and your body position as you go over the bar. The more force you can apply toward the ground through good arm movement at the takeoff, the better jumping action you can create off the ground. Throughout the takeoff, try to accelerate your arm and leg action off the ground and upward, so that your right leg and both arms are as high as you can lift them when the takeoff (left) foot leaves the ground. As you take off, don't let your right knee rotate around and forward of your takeoff leg. This will cause too much body rotation to the bar. The upward drive and the curved run cause you to turn your back

Plant position for the power jumper.
If you are a power jumper, your penultimate step should be slightly shorter than the previous steps (A, B). This lengthens your last stride, lowering your center of gravity and allowing you to drive powerfully straight up and over the bar (C, D). Plant your heel in line with the takeoff standard.

C   B   A

to the bar naturally as you rise off the ground. Let the rotation happen. Don't force it.

Try to keep your body straight, your arms and legs moving upward, and your speed accelerating. Once you go into the takeoff, keep your mind on it. Too many young jumpers switch to thinking about what to do at the top of the bar and lose height on their jumps as a result. Don't cut your takeoff short—keep your speed and momentum going through it. You are going for vertical height at the takeoff, so try to gain as much height as you can. You'll have time to bring your body under control to clear the bar once the height is attained.

Phase Five: The Jump

In the early days of the Flop, every jumper tried to use a double-arm takeoff, in which both arms came up to about chin level and stopped, or "blocked," in that position. This was, and is still, a great way to jump, as it allows you to direct a lot of force downward, toward the ground, and then return this force upward as you block and take off.

There are two other basic arm styles when high jumping. In the first, you continue to raise both arms beyond the chin and let your inside (right) arm lead up and over the bar. This technique allows you to get slightly better lift, as it can help raise your center of gravity just a little higher on takeoff; it can also help you arch your back better when going over the bar.

The other technique, often used by high school girls and developing jumpers, is to reach immediately over the bar with the inside arm. This is easy to perform at low heights, but I don't recommend it. When you start going for greater heights, you'll find that it limits the amount of vertical force that you can attain on takeoff and causes you to lean into the bar too early.

How you approach the bar also affects your arm technique over it. In order to achieve proper arm action at takeoff, you should not run parallel to the bar on your last two strides. If you happen to use the unrecommended single-arm technique and are parallel to the bar, you will have to jump toward the bar, rather than vertically, to get over it. If you use the double-arm technique and are parallel to the bar, you'll have to thrust your arms over the bar, which will both take away from your vertical lift and cause you to rotate too much.

A common mistake that many young jumpers make is to turn the back to the bar at takeoff. If your back is to the bar at takeoff, you lose good vertical lift. Remember, vertical lift first, rotate second. Also: keep your drive knee up during the jump. Do not let it fall.

Double-Arm Techniques at the Takeoff

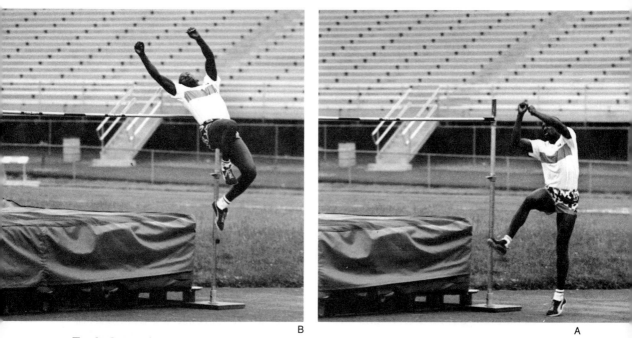

B   A

Technique 1.

At the jump phase, many high jumpers raise both arms over the head (A) and let the inside (right) arm lead over the bar (B).

Technique 2.

Beginners often reach immediately over the bar with their inside arm (A, B). While fine for low heights, this technique limits the amount of vertical force you can attain at takeoff.

A   B

Phase Six: Clearing the Bar

No matter what kind of jumping style you use—single-arm lift, double-arm lift, power jump, speed jump—the best layout position going over the bar is one in which the largest possible amount of your body's mass is below the level of the crossbar at the height of your jump. In other words, your head and upper body clear the bar and drop below its level, and your legs attain the greatest height in the jump as they clear the bar.

After you leave the ground, work at keeping your inside leg up as long as possible. A moment earlier, during your takeoff and reach for the bar, your arms were moving upward. Now, if you performed a double-arm lift, they must move down slightly toward your hips. Moving your arms this way will allow you to raise your hips high over the bar and attain a strong hang position on top of it.

If you reach with one arm, keep it moving over the bar and then down slightly in order to get a good arch.

Keep your heels together as best you can, and your knees apart. Keep your head in good alignment with your back and do not allow it to drop too far back. Whatever you do, do not look back at the inside standard. If you feel comfortable looking past the far standard, you might not experience any problems, but I still recommend turning only slightly toward the far standard.

Once your hips have cleared the bar, raise your legs by flexing your upper body at the hips. This leg-lifting action causes an equal and opposite reaction in the upper body. Many jumpers try to make this a fast movement, or they pike at the waist to bring the legs up, but I don't recommend these techniques, especially when you're going for greater heights. The best movement for lifting the legs is to bend at the waist slightly and bring your head up toward your chest as your legs lift. If you find that you have plenty of bar clearance but are hitting the bar with your ankles on the way down, it means you are attaining your height too late. Try to attain it earlier, before too much of your body mass has gone over the bar.

C B A

Clearing the bar.

This critical phase of the jump begins, after takeoff, by keeping your inside (right) leg up and level with your hips as long as possible (A). The arms, which were upraised on takeoff, move down toward the hips, allowing you to raise your hips high over the bar. As you lower your arms and your hips rise, your heels should be as close together as you can bring them, with your knees apart (B). Note here how the jumper's head has already dropped below the plane of the bar. Once your hips have cleared the bar, raise your legs by flexing your upper body at the hips (C). If you have timed the leg-lift properly, your body should clear the bar without your ankles hitting it.

Phase Seven: The Landing

The key to landing after a high jump is simple: You should land on your entire back, not just your upper back or shoulders, and you should try to keep your legs straight and at a right angle to your torso (an "L" position). Try to land near the middle of the pit, and avoid somersaulting. Once you've landed, you should be able to spring up onto your feet and walk out of the pit.

The landing.
Try to land your jump on your entire back, and keep your body in an "L" position.

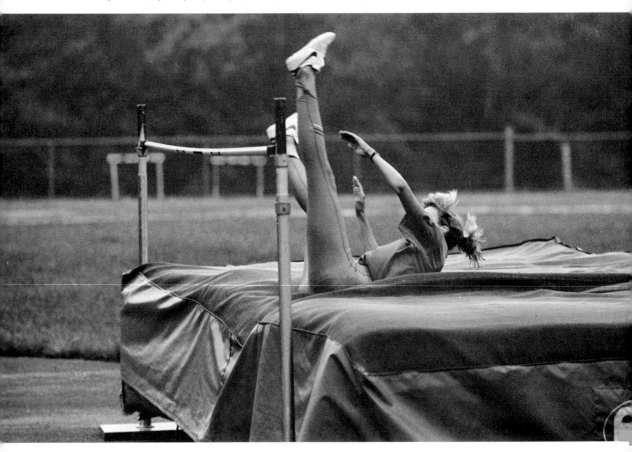

- Too short an approach, preventing you from attaining enough speed into the plant and takeoff. *Solution:* Experiment with lengthening your approach by several strides.

- Inconsistent first step, leading to bad approach steps. *Solution:* Discover the optimum length of your first stride and stick with it. Mark that first step.

- Slowing down when entering the curve phase of your approach. *Solution:* Think "accelerate" as you enter the turn.

- Not accelerating or even maintaining speed through the last three steps. *Solution:* Again, think "accelerate." Also work on your arm action.

- Running parallel to the bar during the last two steps. *Solution:* The curved part of your run should bring you to the bar at an angle, not parallel to it. Check your arc, which ideally should be a segment of a circle, not of an ellipse or an oval. Reduce the length of the arc.

- Taking off too far down the bar and landing off the pit. *Solution:* Remember, you should execute your takeoff at or parallel to the near standard, not out toward the middle of the bar.

- Jumping with your back to the bar on the takeoff. *Solution:* Concentrate on good inward lean during the last few steps of your approach and on making a good plant for the takeoff. Both will help you rotate your back naturally toward the bar at the proper moment. Also, try to keep your inside shoulder higher than your outside shoulder.

- Planting your foot parallel to the bar for takeoff. *Solution:* Keep your arc circular, and make your plant pointing to the inside of the far standard.

- Leaning with the inside shoulder (the one nearest the bar) down on the takeoff. *Solution:* Strive to keep your inside shoulder somewhat higher than the outside. If your approach to the bar is fast enough, your inside shoulder should tend to be higher anyway.

- Dropping the free leg too soon after takeoff. *Solution:* Keep the free knee up until you are at the peak of your takeoff.

- "Sitting" on top of the bar. *Solution:* Move your hands to your sides as you start to clear the bar, and after your upper body is over, raise your hips.

- Not getting good height in front of the bar. *Solution:* Work on your approach, plant, takeoff, and arm reach. Be patient. Take your Flop apart; look at each segment with your coach; and carefully, deliberately, put it back together again.

G   F   E   D

N   M   L

Putting It All Together: The High Jump

C   B   A

K   J   I   H

Four steps into his nine-step approach run, this high jumper has everything under control. He begins his leftward lean into the arc (A). As he makes his fifth (B, C), sixth (D, E), and seventh (F) steps, he continues to accelerate through the arc. Since he is a power jumper, his penultimate step is a shorter one (G, H), causing his last stride to be longer, which lowers his center of gravity (I) for takeoff (J). Note the position of the arms and the right leg, and that the heel is in line with the standard. The jumper tries to keep his right leg up for as long as possible as the arms, head, and upper body start to clear the bar (K). By moving his hands down slightly toward his hips, the jumper is able to raise his hips over the bar. Meanwhile his heels are together and his knees remain apart (L). Once his hips have cleared the bar, the jumper raises his legs by flexing his upper body at the hips (M). Legs cleared, he drops into the pit on his full back, his body in the "L" shape (N). A successful jump!

DRILLS FOR THE HIGH JUMP

Plyometric Jumps. Single- and double-leg hops for height.

Upward Jumps while holding a light barbell or pair of light barbells.

Step Jumps, hopping up and down on one step, with either or both feet.

Hopping Down Stairs (a great preseason drill).

Imitation Drills for Takeoff. Jump into the air as if going for a bar. Do not use the pit. Jump up and land back on your feet.

Jumping over Hurdles with both legs: 10 low hurdles, 6 to 8 times.

Ankle Drills. Extend your body as if going for a bar, using only your ankles for leverage. This action places a big load on your calf muscles and balls of your feet, strengthening both.

Technique Jumps over a Low Bar: 15 to 20 jumps with full run. Work on all aspects of jumping technique.

Technique Jumps over a High Bar: 8 to 10 jumps with full run.

Abdominal Work in the weight room (see pages 108–111).

Jump over Bar using scissors technique.

Check-mark Drills, checking step and takeoff points.

Circle Runs: running in a circle of the same radius as your approach, to help develop proper lean and stride length in the arc.

Standing Arm and Free Leg Imitation Drills. Stand on your takeoff foot and drive your arms and free knee upward as if taking off for a jump.

Pop-ups Without the Bar, Short Approach. The aim of this drill is to help you develop a good plant, arm action, and vertical takeoff. Your approach need only be 3 to 5 steps, but it should be on the arc. Practice your plant, arm action, and takeoff without actually following through with the jump. See how high you can pop up on each plant. Five to 10 jumps is sufficient.

Arc Approach. Approach the bar using only the arc that you normally use. Instead of using 5 steps, use 7 steps.

Double-Arm Vertical Skips to develop an explosive takeoff. Skip from one foot to the other, trying to attain as much vertical height as you can off each foot. As you skip, move your arms forcefully together, just as you would during a plant and takeoff. Skip for 30 yards; rest 30 seconds; skip again. Do 10 to 12 skips at a time.

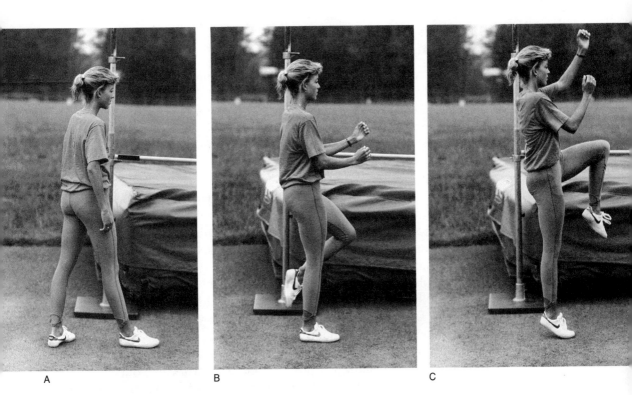

A   B   C

The standing arm and free leg imitation drill.
You can do this drill anywhere. Its purpose is to program your arm and leg action at takeoff so that it becomes automatic. Start by stepping onto your takeoff foot, your heel in line with the standard (A). Then drive your inside leg and your arms upward as you would for a takeoff (B, C).

Double-Leg Back Jumps. Jump backward with both legs over a distance of 10 yards a set; rest; repeat. Do 3 sets of back jumps per session.

Short-Approach Jumps over the Bar. Keep the bar low and your approach short—maybe five or six steps along the arc. Work on your plant and takeoff, paying particular attention to your arm and hip action upward and over the bar.

COMPETITION: HOW TO PREPARE FOR IT
AND PERFORM YOUR BEST

Competition adds a whole new dimension to the high-jumping experience—one that can bring you a great deal of self-knowledge and personal satisfaction. Here are some suggestions and reminders that may help make the competitive experience fun, challenging, and rewarding.

• In practice, work on improving your concentration. Then use what you've worked on in meets.

• In both practice and competition, walk to the bar. Measure out your approach. Place the bar an inch or more above your personal best and walk through your approach, thinking about jumping over this new height. Feel yourself leaning into the bar. Feel your plant and takeoff. Picture yourself clearing this great height today!

• Repeat the plant, using your foot and arms. Feel how the plant must be for your jump to be successful. What are the forces that come into play on a successful plant? Lock into those forces, and picture yourself locking into them when you make your actual jump.

• Before performing a competitive (or even a practice) jump, mentally rehearse it on the field, by yourself if possible. Learn to work by yourself on the practice field. In competition, when you are at the head of the apron, you are by yourself. Rehearse this feeling. Picture yourself in this place. Practice it mentally and physically.

• In competition, do some slight warming-up movements prior to each jump. Do not sit and wait for your name to be called, and then stand up and jump. Get both mind and body ready for the jump. Always know where you are in the jumping order.

• In competition jumpers get only 90 seconds to jump once their name is called. Ninety seconds is not much time, so you need to prepare for each attempt prior to that 90-second period.

• When making an attempt, think only of the positive. What phase of the jump do you do best? What are the strengths of your approach or plant? If you think "I need to correct this or that movement because it makes me jump poorly," you run a greater risk of a poor jump because of a negative thought. Instead, stay intent, but be relaxed and think positive. Focus on what you do best!

• During your warm-ups before a competition, take some jumps at a high height. Do not wait for the competition before getting your first look at that height. Tell the judges precisely where you want the bar set, and then go for it.

- Concentrate on each jump and give every one your best effort.
- As the bar goes higher in competition or practice, do you need to change heights within yourself? Understand what you need of yourself at higher heights and practice those movements and thoughts at home, on the practice field, and in meets.

Whenever you're competing, make a strong effort to clear the bar on your first attempt. Many jumpers overlook the fact that if they succeed in their first attempt, they put a great deal of pressure on the other jumpers. But you must be ready to make that jump, mentally as well as physically.

At the 1983 World Championships, the three medalists in the men's high jump made 17 successful jumps in the final. Of these, 9 were made on first attempts, 2 were made on second attempts, and only 1 was made on the third attempt.

The top three women at the 1983 World Championships had 20 successful attempts: 15 on first attempts, 5 on second attempts, and none on third attempts. The message of these statistics is clear: Don't hold back. Make that first jump, and every one thereafter, a success.

During your training sessions, place the bar at heights well above your personal best. Attempt several jumps at those heights, working for clearance every time you jump. Take note of your mental attitude toward these jumps. Do you really try to make them, or do you just go through the motions? Going through the motions—in any endeavor—will never help you improve or succeed. Really go for it.

The last suggestion I can offer is to to start jumping early in a competition. Remember, you can enter a high-jump competition at any height you want. I suggest you come in early, at a low height, and work your way up. Especially if you're a beginning or intermediate jumper, one of the worst things you can do is to start your competition at a high height and put lots of pressure on yourself to make it as an opener. To me that's like gambling. Sure, maybe you can make that high opening height, but if you can't, you'll soon find yourself putting on your sweats and watching others compete. Jump early!

COACHING TIPS FOR THE HIGH JUMP

- Make sure the jumper establishes a nine- or ten-step approach.
- Be sure the jumper's arc phase is only five steps.
- Watch to make sure the jumper initiates the arc (last five steps) on the

outside foot. For example, if the jumper's left is his takeoff foot, he should also start his arc with his left foot.

• Emphasize to the jumper the importance of good speed through the approach run, and proper lean through the arc.

• Does the jumper accelerate into the last three steps of the approach? He should.

• Watch where the jumper plants his takeoff foot. It should be almost parallel to the near standard, about 24 to 30 inches out from the bar, and pointing toward the far standard. It should *not* be planted parallel to the bar.

• The jumper should use both arms, in coordination with the inside knee, for an aggressive upward drive. Be sure the jumper drives the knee at a 90-degree angle on the lift-off.

• When in the air, the jumper should not drop the inside knee. Stress keeping the knee up!

• Watch the jumper's head during the actual jump. It should be turned slightly toward the far standard.

• A good landing occurs in the middle, or slightly beyond the middle, of the pit. The jumper should never land near the outside edge of the pit.

SAMPLE TRAINING WEEKS FOR THE HIGH JUMP

The workouts here should give you a good idea of the number of training options open to you and your teammates. As you'll discover, training your legs to run and jump takes time, and there are many ways to train. If you can work indoors during bad weather, your progress will be quicker. But don't take shortcuts; if you want to be a good jumper you have to train, and train properly.

The Off-Season (October–February)

Monday

Warm-up.
Stride: 200 meters, 5 to 8 times.
Uphill runs for power: 40 meters, 5 to 8 times.
Downhill runs.
Stretching exercises.
Cool-down.

Warm-up.
Weight work in the weight room:

Exercise	Sets	Reps
Full squats	4	5
Power cleans	4	5
Leg extensions	3	8
Leg curls	3	8
Hip flexors	3	3–3–3
Body curls	2	10
Biceps curls	3	8
Split squats	4	8–12
Jump squats	4	8–12
Step-ups with weights	4	8–12
Dumbbell sprints with weights	4	30 sec.

Stretch.
Cool-down.

Wednesday

Warm-up.
150-meter sprints, accelerating at the end: 5 times.
Upper body plyometrics: 20 min.
Bounding exercises: 30–40 meters, 20 min.
Cool-down.

Thursday

Warm-up.
50-meter sprints, accelerating at the end: 5 times.
Weight room workout (follow Tuesday schedule).
Stretch.
Cool-down.

Friday

Warm-up: 20 min.
Uphill runs: 40 meters.
Downhill runs: 40 meters.

Upper body plyometrics: 30 min.
300-meter runs at 80% effort (run for form).
Cool-down.

Pre-Season (March)

Monday

Warm-up: 20 min.
Technique jumps at low height, using short runs: 30 min.
Long approach runs, jumping at low height, working on form: 30 min.
Weight room work.
Cool-down: 10–12 min.

Tuesday

Warm-up: 20 min.
Plyometrics: 40–45 min.
Cool-down: 10–12 min.

Wednesday

Warm-up.
75-meter sprints, accelerating: 5 times.
Stretching: 15 min.
Weight room work.
Cool-down: 10 min.

Thursday

Warm-up: 20 min.
Short approach runs at the bar, using scissor takeoffs: 20 min.
Short approach runs, working on approach and takeoff, low bar: 30 min.
Long approach runs, working on technique, low–medium bar: 20 min.
Upper body plyometrics: 15 min.
Cool-down.

Friday

Warm-up: 20 min.
Plyometrics: 30 min.
Weight room work: 60 min.
Cool-down.

Competitive Season (April–June)

Monday

Warm-up: 20 min.
30-meter sprints for acceleration: 3 times.
Scissor jumps, low bar: 5 times.
Technique jumps, low bar: 20–25 times, short approach run.
Weight work: 40–50 min.

Tuesday

Warm-up: 20 min.
Bounding: 35–45 meters, 40 min.
Upper body plyometrics: 20 min.
Stretch.
Cool-down.

Wednesday

Warm-up: 20 min.
Weight work: 50–60 min.
Stretch.
Cool-down: 10–12 min.

Thursday

Warm-up: 20 min.
Low jumps, full approach: 4–5 times.
Jump for height: no more than 8 times. (Take the last 2 jumps at least 2 in.
  above your best height. This is a quality workout, and your mental and
  physical skills should be developed greatly.
Light bounding: 20 min.
Cool-down.

Friday

Warm-up: Jog and walk, 20 min.
Stretching: 20 min.
Jog: 15 min.

Saturday

Competition day. Start low, and work your way up through the jumps.

5

The Long Jump

What does it take to become a good long jumper? In a word: speed. If you can sprint, you can jump. You'll find that often the best long jumpers—at every level from high school to the Olympics—also run on sprint relay teams. These athletes may be short or tall, but their speed makes them desirable both as sprinters and as long jumpers.

GETTING STARTED IN THE LONG JUMP

The object of long jumping is to take a running start, hit the takeoff board without stepping beyond it, and leap as far as possible into the pit. The distance of the jump is measured from the pit side of the takeoff board to the nearest mark in the sand made by any part of your body.

Your approach run can be as long or as short as you wish, but most runs will be between 100 and 120 feet. The takeoff board, which is 2 meters from the landing pit, is set flush with the ground and measures 4 feet by 8 inches. The landing pit is filled with sand and measures 9 by 26 feet.

If you've never long-jumped seriously before, start to learn the proper technique by performing the following drills:

1. Skip on the track for about 40 meters. Repeat 3 or 4 times. On each repeat, try to raise your knees higher and lengthen the distance of the skips. For example, your first few skips may be for a distance of only 2 feet or so. As you raise your knees higher, you will travel a little farther on each skip, perhaps

At the 1968 Olympics in Mexico City, Bob Beamon set a world record in the long jump of 29 feet 2 inches. The record still stands—a testament to one of the world's greatest sports achievements.

3 to 4 feet at a time. When you perform this exercise, keep your back straight and swing your arms forcefully.

2. Now go over to the long-jump pit. Rake it smooth, making sure there is no debris in the sand, and get ready to jump.

3. Starting about 25 feet from the edge of the sand pit, begin a slow run. When you are close to the end of the runway, jump into the air. Try to land on one foot, and after you land, run out of the pit. If you are right-handed, take off from your left foot, extend your right foot out over the pit, land on the right foot, and then run out of the pit. Repeat this drill several times.

4. Now go back to your starting point and take another run, but this time, as you jump off your left foot and extend your right leg out over the pit, quickly bring your left foot up to the right. Land with both feet close together and bounce forward out of the pit.

Developing Your Distance

1. To have some fun as you start to get the hang of extending with one foot on the jump and bringing the other foot up alongside it, set a towel out in the pit, and see if you can jump over it on all your jumps. Do not try to take off on the jumping board until you feel comfortable executing a jump with the forward-bouncing landing. Just take off from the end of the runway and have some fun jumping. Once you feel comfortable, you're ready to start practicing the more technical aspects of long jumping.

2. Set a 12-inch-high parking cone in the pit at a distance you know you can jump comfortably (if you can jump 20 feet, set the cone at 19 feet). Jump over the cone, working on a consistent landing pattern. Every three weeks, move the cone out 3 to 4 inches.

PERFORMING THE LONG JUMP

Determining Your Takeoff Foot

If you are right-handed, your takeoff foot will probably be your left foot. The left foot provides power and stability on the takeoff. However, if after taking some short runs, you find that you can take off with more spring from your right foot, and if it feels comfortable during the transition from the run to the takeoff, by all means use the right foot.

Developing the Approach for the Jump

The approach run in the long jump is really the key to your performance. If your run is short and you are not able to generate enough speed down the runway, you will find it difficult to convert that reduced speed into a good lift-off and flight through the air. Remember, long jumps begin with speed!

Many jumpers like to take short runs of about 20 to 30 feet and then take what's known as a pop-up jump into the pit. Short runs are suitable occasionally for drilling in the takeoff, flight, and landing, but they really don't give you the necessary practice that a full run does. You will often hear coaches advise their jumpers to "run off the board" or "sprint off the board," which is exactly what a good approach will do for you. A good approach will allow you to sprint off the board and give you time in the air to prepare for a good landing far out into the pit. Your run should be long enough to allow you to gain maximum speed as you hit the takeoff board because, again, the whole point of the takeoff is to convert horizontal speed into jumping distance.

How long your approach should be depends on your speed and strength. I recommend the following distances as general measurements:

Beginners: 90 to 100 feet, 13 to 15 strides

Intermediates: 100 to 110 feet, 15 to 17 strides

Advanced: 110 to 120 feet or longer, 17 to 19 strides

Another way to gauge the length of your approach run is to count your strides. As a beginner, you may want to take only a 13- to 15-stride approach. If you are an intermediate jumper (a boy who can jump over 20 feet or a girl who can jump over 16 feet), you may want to take from 15 to 17 strides. As an advanced jumper (a boy who can jump over 22 feet or a girl who can jump over 18 feet), you should work on developing a 19- to 21-stride approach—or more—depending on your ability to sustain a sprint over a long distance. Don't measure your steps until well into the season. The length of your strides will change as your sprinting technique improves, so you should measure them about two weeks into the training season.

The Speed of the Run
During the Approach

One of the biggest mistakes that young jumpers make is to start with a short run and then sprint as fast as they can over that short distance, trying to gain speed for a good jump. By doing that, these jumpers never give themselves the chance of gaining full speed under control. In addition, the short distance impedes good sprint technique down the runway.

The more I watch successful high school, collegiate, and world-class jumpers, the more I notice that they all tend to start down the runway at a slow but controlled pace, and gradually build their speed over the entire distance of the run. This is true of both male and female jumpers, and I am convinced that their slow starts help them attain good sprint speed by the end of their runs. Remember, the more relaxed you are down the runway, the easier it will be for you to attain good sprint form and speed. You can relax your run if you allow yourself good distance in the approach.

How to Sprint
Down the Runway

Start your approach with short steps, and extend the length of your stride as you pick up speed. If your first step is too long, you'll get into the sprint phase of your approach too soon, which will cause you to decelerate a bit just before takeoff.

Use your arms to help control your speed. Start with your arms low, and as you pick up speed and start to accelerate into good sprinting form, move your arms the way a sprinter does—straight ahead, not across the body—and maintain an erect body position. Keep your head in alignment with your spine, and look ahead at the long jump pit, *not* at the takeoff board. Look beyond the board.

Coaches tell me that there are three crucial factors in long-jumping successfully: speed, ability to relax, and exactitude (the ability to maintain exact running and jumping technique). We know that speed is critical, and your ability to relax as you sprint is the key to good speed. But both of these factors are of no value if you step over the toe board and foul on your jump. You must be able to plant your takeoff foot within 1 inch of the front edge of the takeoff board in order to gain any benefit from your sprint. That is what is meant by being exact. Think of it this way: Good jumping starts by being able to run a distance of 100 or more feet, sprint the last few yards as fast as you can, and then plant your foot at a point within 1 inch of the end of the board. In other words, good jumping requires being able to sprint 99 feet 11 inches every time you try. If you can do that (and few can), consider yourself a very consistent jumper.

To develop consistency, you must learn to know how you feel when you sprint. What is going on in the muscles of your arms, legs, chest, neck, back, and abdomen? What movements does your body go through from the start through the transition to the full sprint and takeoff phases? The only way to begin to answer these questions is to sprint, to think about sprinting, and to learn about the person you are as you sprint. What speeds and stride lengths can you handle effectively? What is your maximum controlled sprint speed? Have you ever just "fallen out" or "fallen apart" when you ran too fast? What exactly happened then?

The Approach Strides

Using check marks is essential in helping you take exact approach strides. The idea is to establish how far up the runway you should begin your run and where your feet should hit, so that you arrive at the takeoff on the proper foot and well prepared to jump. This measuring can be done either on the runway or on the track. You will need a tape measure at least 150 feet long and, ideally, a coach or observer who can watch where your feet land and mark accordingly.

Let's say that you feel relatively comfortable with a 15-stride approach that covers a distance of roughly 100 feet. Measure 100 feet from the front of the toe board and call the point "S" (start). If you take off on your actual jump from your left foot, S marks the starting position of your right foot.

Begin to accelerate slowly down the runway, first counting the strides of your left foot (takeoff foot), which is the first to move out from your standing position. On its eighth stride, your left foot should hit squarely on the toe board; then you go into your takeoff into the jump. Check to see where your eighth stride actually hits (remember, this is a trial-and-error process). If your left foot's eighth stride is 3 feet in front of the board, for example, move the starting point closer by 3 feet, to 97 feet.

Now we come to the key for obtaining good stride length. Start at 100 feet and have your observer mark the spot where you make the second step with your left foot. This should be 10 to 11 feet from S, or 90 or 89 feet from the toe board. Mark this point; call it check mark "B." This mark indicates where your second left step should occur every time you make your approach—*if* you accelerate comfortably, slowly, and smoothly from your starting position. Check mark B should always remain the same, no matter what the jumping circumstances. It is an exact point of reference you should shoot for when working on your approach, and should always be your first concern as you start your approach run. When training or competing, be sure to put a good marker at this check point: a shoe, towel, number marker, or piece of tape will suffice so long as it's clearly visible and doesn't blow away. During every practice week, take the time to practice this part of your approach so that you become consistent at hitting this mark.

As you practice your approaches and find that you are hitting the board correctly at 100 feet using a total of 15 strides, check mark B becomes a handy reference point for guaranteeing a proper approach. If, after a while, you find that your tenth left-foot stride is going over the board by a certain distance (which often happens as a jumper's sprint technique improves), move both your starting mark (S) and your second left step mark (B) back by that same distance.

As you approach the moment of takeoff, concentrate on good sprinting technique and on running at full speed when you hit the board. The last four strides should be your fastest, and you should picture yourself sprinting right to and off the board. You may have heard coaches say to "settle" or "relax"

A 15-step approach.
In a 15-step approach where the jumper takes off from the board on his left foot, the left foot makes 8 strides, the right foot 7. Note the position of check mark B: at the point where the left foot makes its second stride. Once you find yourself hitting the board with consistency, check mark B becomes an important reference point for ensuring proper stride length.

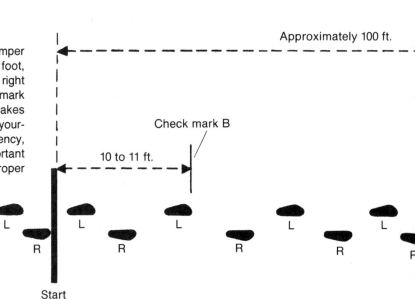

as you hit the last four strides, but this is exactly the opposite of what you want to do. Be like a sprinter in a close race and sprint through the takeoff board as if it were a finish line.

If you find that you are fouling on jumps (stepping over the toe board), it is probably because you are not sprinting at full speed and are losing your rhythm over the last few strides. Slowing down causes you to lengthen your last few strides and thus foul. The solution lies not in adjusting the marks, but in thinking like a sprinter so that you run *through* the board and don't slow down to get *to* it. Should you stamp your takeoff foot on the board? No, simply plant your foot naturally on the board; this will give you a good lift off the board. Should your eyes focus down on the board as you near it? Yes, but only slightly. Keep looking beyond the board.

Regarding the plant: You will find that you want to lengthen your next-to-last stride somewhat to lower your center of gravity, then make your last stride quick as you can to the board. The last stride will be shorter than the penultimate stride by 4 to 6 inches. The effect is to lift your center of gravity as you touch the board and to continue that lift into the actual jump. Good striding at the end of an approach makes jumping fun; you propel yourself into the air and *go for it!*

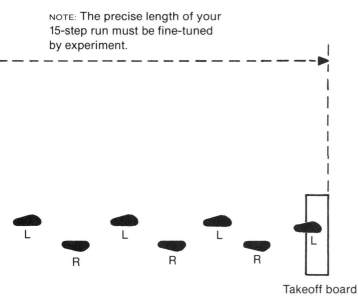

NOTE: The precise length of your 15-step run must be fine-tuned by experiment.

L   R   L   R   L   R   L   L

Takeoff board

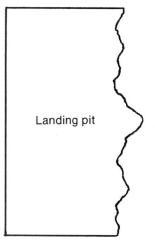

Landing pit

The Takeoff

Remember, do not slow down at the end of the run; instead, sprint through the takeoff board. Do not chop (shorten) your steps to find the right lengths into the takeoff. Accelerate as you near the board.

The heel of the takeoff foot should hit first, at the front edge of the board, so that the foot rolls over the board and you can drive off it with good speed and power. Come off the board with your head up and your back straight. As you start to come off the board, think like a hurdler going into the hurdles: that is, make a strong forward punch with your free knee upward and outward. The punch must lift and lead the body and prevent the body from leaning out over the legs.

If your free leg is your right leg (the left foot is your takeoff foot), drive your left elbow up and out over the pit with as much force as you can generate. Think elbow and not arm, as this will help give you a faster and better overall lift position off the board. If you can get your free knee and left elbow moving in the proper direction at the takeoff, you will attain the proper 20- to 25-degree angle for your flight path through the air. Meanwhile, don't worry about your right elbow. It will move back naturally as you drive your left elbow forward.

Action in the Air

If your takeoff is smooth, fast, and correct, what you do thereafter, while you are in flight, will determine the length of your jump. If your action in the air is correct, you can extend your landing 6 to 12 inches; if it is poor, you can lose 6 to 15 inches. Two styles in flight are the Hang and the 1½-Step Hitchkick. Properly executed, each can affect the length of the jump, though their primary purpose is to get your arms and legs in position for landing. The Hang is probably the easier to learn, and I recommend it especially to beginners. As you take off, bring the trailing leg alongside the lead leg, knees apart and slightly bent. Your arms are raised, and until the midpoint of the jump, you should appear to be hanging from a trapeze. Then bring your arms forward forcefully, which raises your legs and brings them forward as well, and get ready to land.

The Hitchkick takes greater coordination. At takeoff the lead knee comes to hip height, followed by the takeoff leg, which comes through as though you were running in the air, followed by the lead leg again so that both legs are now in an extended position in front. Keeping your arms straight, windmill them to help rotate your legs. I would not recommend the Hitchkick to either boys or girls unless they can jump at least 22 feet.

The Takeoff

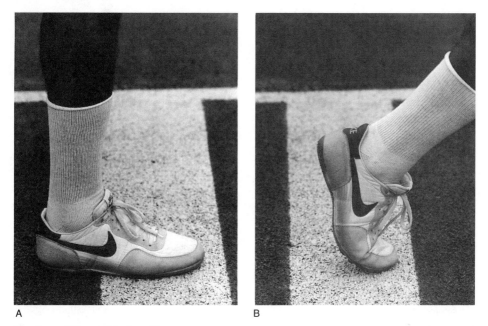

A   B

Foot position at takeoff.
The heel of the takeoff foot hits first, at the front edge of the board (A), allowing the foot to roll over the board (B) so that you can drive off with good speed and power.

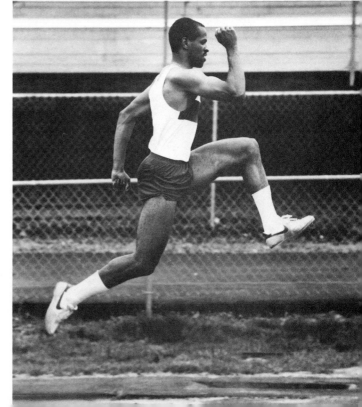

Body position at takeoff.
This jumper takes off on his right foot, and here, his body position at takeoff is excellent. His back is straight; he has made a strong punch, forward and outward, with his free (left) knee; and his opposite (right) elbow is up and forward like a sprinter's.

A

B

The Hang. (above)

For this method of flight, bring your trailing leg alongside the lead leg as you take off (A, B). As your legs come together, the knees should be close together and slightly bent, and your arms should be raised over your head (C). Until the midpoint of the jump, you should appear to be hanging from a trapeze (D). Now bring your arms forward forcefully, which raises your legs and brings them forward (E). Let your arms sweep past your legs as you land. The Hang is an excellent technique for all jumpers, and the easiest technique to learn.

A

B

C

D

E

The Hitchkick. (below)
For this method of flight, the lead knee at takeoff comes to hip height (A). Then the takeoff leg comes forward as though you were running in air (B, C), followed by the takeoff leg (D), so that going into the landing both legs are in an extended position in front (E). Note, throughout the Hitchkick, how the arms windmill to help rotate the legs.

C

D

E

One training aid in learning to gain height is to suspend a towel or a sponge from a pole-vault standard at the midpoint of the jump, a little over 10 feet off the ground. As you take off, try to touch the towel with your head.

Landing

The aim in landing is to touch down with your feet as far forward as possible and not to fall backward and leave marks in the sand behind your feet. Therefore, your center of gravity must pass over and beyond your feet, but only at the last possible moment—too early and you'll land too soon, robbing yourself of several inches or feet of distance. Your arms should reach forward over your feet as if you were coming out of a forward roll and continue sweeping past your hips so that when you land, your hands will actually be behind your hips. Your heels break the sand, and your knees flex outward as your hips pass between your knees. Keep your momentum moving forward as you exit the landing pit.

COACHING TIPS FOR THE LONG JUMP

- Make sure the jumper uses a 17- to 21-step approach to the board.
- Help the jumper establish an accurate check mark for the start, and use a second check mark to establish the location for the second step of the left foot.
- Watch to be sure the jumper accelerates slowly from the start.
- The jumper should build up approach speed gradually, and go aggressively into the last five steps of the approach. He or she should not slow down or "settle into" the board.
- The jumper's second-to-last step (the penultimate step) should be long, and the last step 4 to 6 inches shorter. The jumper's body should lower on the penultimate step, and then rise up on the last step onto the board.
- Watch the jumper's knee and arm action on takeoff. The free knee should drive up and out vigorously, as should the opposite elbow. The jumper's back should be straight and erect, keeping the head up.
- If the jumper cannot jump more than 22 feet, urge him or her to use the Hang style of jumping.
- Study the jumper's landing. When his feet touch down, his arms should be sweeping down and back, behind the hips.
- Have the jumper strive for speed by training with the team's sprinters. The goal is to gain as much controlled speed as possible down the runway.
- Have the jumper practice approach runs as often as possible, without jumping. During competition, he or she should strive to be able to hit the board on every attempt.
- Put your jumpers on the relay teams.

The Landing

A good landing begins with your feet far forward and your arms reaching forward, beyond the feet (A). Your arms continue sweeping past your hips so that when you land, your hands are behind your hips. Your heels break the sand, and your knees flex outward as your hips move forward (B). Your momentum continues to move forward as you exit the landing pit (C).

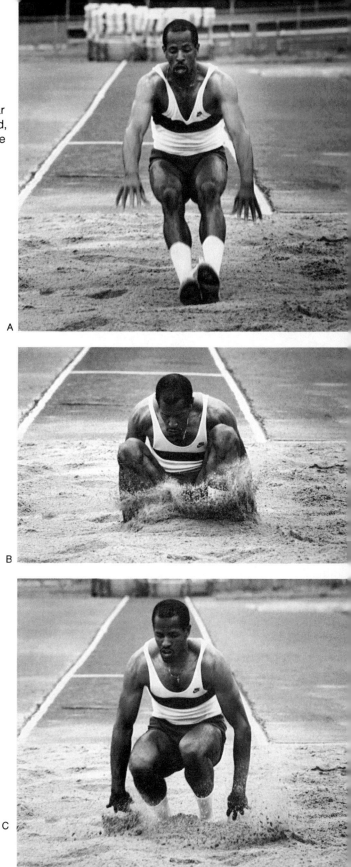

A

B

C

Putting It All Together: The Long Jump

A

B

E

F

C

D

G

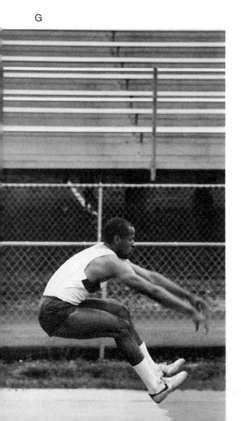

A successful long jump begins with a controlled, steadily accelerating approach of 13 to 19 strides (100 to 120 feet) (A). After a long penultimate step (B), the takeoff step is somewhat shorter (C). At the takeoff, the jumper's lead knee drives up and out, and his lead arm drives up, like a sprinter's (D). At takeoff, for an effective Hang action through the air, the trailing leg comes up alongside the lead leg, the knees remain close together, and the arms are raised as if the jumper is hanging from a trapeze (E). The jumper holds the hang through the midpoint of his jump (F), then extends his arms and legs forward for the landing (G).

SAMPLE TRAINING WEEKS
FOR THE LONG JUMP

These workouts are samples that may give you some idea of the variety of things you can do to have fun while you develop good jumping skills.

The Off-Season (October–February)

Monday

Warm-up: 20 min.
Running drills:
  Uphill runs
  Pace running: 200 meters at 95%, 5–8 times
Cool-down.

Tuesday

Warm-up: 20 min.
Weight work:

Exercise	Sets	Reps
Squats with weights	3–5	6–12
Half squats, rising on toes	3–5	6–12
Leg curls	2–3	10–12
Leg extensions	2	10–12
Step-ups	2	10–12
Split squats	3–5	8–12
Jump squats	2–3	8–12
Dumbbell sprint action	3	30 sec.

Cool-down.

Wednesday

Warm-up.
Light runs for form: 150–200 meters 5 times.
Upper body plyometrics.
Cool-down.

Thursday

Warm-up.
Standing long jumps: 6 times.
Standing two-hop jump: 6 times.
Standing hops, right leg, left leg: 6 times.
50-meter sprints for acceleration: 5 times.
Jog: 20 min.

Friday

Warm-up.
Easy running: 15 min.
50-meter running drills, acclerating: 6 times.
Standing jumps: 6 times.
Standing step-and-hop: 6 times.
Standing triple-jump drills: 6 times.
Weight work.

Pre-Season (March)

Monday

Warm-up.
Easy running: 10 min.
50-meter running drills: 6 times.
Work on step for the approach in the jump.
60-meter acceleration runs: 6 times.
Weight work: 40 min.
Cool-down.

Tuesday

Warm-up.
Two-thirds full run-ups, with run through the pit: 10–15 times.
Jumps with 10 steps run-up: 3–5 times.
Jumps with 6 steps run-up: 4–6 times.
Bounding plyometrics.
Cool-down.

Wednesday

Warm-up.
Bounding drills: 40 min.
Upper body plyometrics: 20 min.
Light running on grass or soft surface: 15 min.
Work with sprint relay team.
Stretching.
Cool-down.

Thursday

Warm-up.
Work with 4 × 100-meter relay teams.
Box drills for plyometrics: 20 min.
Upper body weight work with dumbbells: 10 min.
Stretching exercises: 20 min.
Cool-down.

Friday

Warm-up.
Standing long jumps: 5 times.
Standing leaps into pit off both feet: 5 times.
Standing bounds off right, then left leg: 5 times.
Full runs to check step for approach: 8 times.
Short runs of 6 steps and take-off: 5 times.
80-meter acceleration sprints: 4 times.
Weight work: 40 min.
Cool-down: 10–12 min.

Competitive Season (April–June)

Monday

Warm-up.
10 bounding running drills: 4 times.
10 takeoffs with 7-step approach. Work on good technique.
10 takeoffs, working on landing. Work on good extension during landing.
80-meter acceleration sprints: 5 times.
Cool-down: 10–12 min.

Warm-up: 20 min.
Bounding drills: 40 min.
Light running: 20 min.
Cool-down: 10–12 min.

Wednesday

Warm-up: 20 min.
Work with relay teams.
Weight work: 60 min.
Cool-down: 10–12 min.

Thursday

Warm-up: 20 min.
Easy strides on grass at 50%: 100 meters, 5 times.
Easy jog: 20 min.
Work with relay teams.
Stretching.
Cool-down: 10–12 min. (This is actually a day of rest.)

Friday

Warm-up.
Light running on grass: 15 min.
Stretching: 20 min.
(This day is also a resting day prior to competition.)

Saturday

Competition day. Take good run-throughs to establish your step. Take at least
one good takeoff to establish a pattern. Be ready for every jump.

6

The Triple Jump

The triple jump used to be called the Hop, Step, and Jump, and in discussing the different phases, we still use those terms. To accomplish this jump, assuming a right-foot takeoff, you push off with the right and come down on the right (the Hop), take off again on the right and come down on the left (the Step), take off on the left and land in the pit on both feet (the Jump). As with the long jump, the triple jump requires a good approach to maintain speed through all three phases.

The event is conducted on a regular long-jump runway and landing pit. The differences are that the takeoff board is set farther back up the runway and the approach run is usually shorter than in the long jump. For international competition the takeoff board is at least 36 feet from the landing area. For beginners or youngsters, 29 feet 6 inches is suggested, or even less if necessary.

Performing the triple jump well requires concentration and practice. Being strong helps, but speed, balance, and rhythm can compensate for a lack of strength. If you are not that strong physically, take heart: working hard on these other physical attributes can make you a fine triple jumper.

GETTING STARTED IN THE TRIPLE JUMP

Talk about having fun with the field events! You'll love getting started in the triple jump. It allows you to run, jump, hop, skip—all the things you used to do in elementary school.

1. Start by skipping on the track for 40 meters. Repeat 3 or 4 times. As

In the triple jump, speed, balance, and rhythm are just as important as strength.

you did in getting started for the long jump, get your knees high and swing your arms forcefully. Get the feeling of hanging in the air.

2. Now stand on your right leg on the track or the grass infield, and take 5 hops. Repeat the drill using your left leg. You'll find that one leg feels stronger than the other. If you are right-handed, you'll usually find that it is easier to hop on your right leg, but this isn't always true.

3. After you can hop for 5 or 6 hops, try doing a standing triple jump. Stand on your right leg, hop up, hop up again, then hop up on your left leg. Do 3 of these drills standing in place: Right-right-left, right-right-left, right-right-left.

4. Repeat the same drill, this time hopping forward instead of standing in place. Try to do at least 3 repetitions in good rhythm, so that you can start to get a sense of proper body balance.

5. Next, switch legs and repeat the drill going left-left-right, left-left-right, left-left-right. Repeat several times, starting with either leg. When you are learning the triple jump, you shouldn't favor one leg over the other.

6. Standing about 15 feet from the edge of the jumping pit, try a triple jump without a run. Stand with both feet together and fall forward (that is, let your upper body lean forward as if you were falling); this starts the momentum of the jump. Then hop right-right-left, jump into the air with both feet, and land in the pit with your feet together. You are now triple-jumping!

7. Repeat this drill several times starting with your right leg; then switch to your left. Now mark a spot about 20 feet from the edge of the pit; this will be the takeoff point for the jump. Move back another 10 to 15 feet; this will be the starting point for your approach run. Take five approach steps, hit your jump point, and go into the triple jump—right-right-left—and finish by jumping into the pit with both feet. Try several jumps. Nice job! Now, with the aid of your coach, you are ready to start learning the actual event.

PERFORMING THE TRIPLE JUMP

Choosing the Takeoff Leg

Now comes the time to decide which leg to use for the takeoff. To make a choice, stand on the grass and hop forward for 10 to 15 meters on your left leg. Repeat the exercise on your right leg. Then repeat the exercise again, this time bringing the hopping leg up high so that your heel almost touches your buttocks before bringing it down for the landing. Which leg gives you more support? With which do you feel most comfortable? Most right-handers find that their right leg gives them more comfort, stability, and speed. If that's the case for you, make the right leg your hopping leg for the triple jump.

The Approach

As in the long jump, the approach in the triple jump is a key to success. You need to be able to generate good speed, but not necessarily all-out speed. You need to run fast enough for a strong hop off the takeoff board, and to keep that speed going through the step and jump phases as well. If you're a beginner, I recommend an approach run of 13 to 15 strides. However, consider the overall length of your run as well, and remember that all-out speed at the end of the approach in the triple jump could be detrimental to your takeoff. Some suggested approach lengths for triple jumpers:

> Beginners: 80 to 100 feet, 13 to 15 strides
>
> Intermediates: 100 to 110 feet, 15 to 17 strides
>
> Advanced: 110 to 120 feet, 17 to 19 strides

The approach must be long enough to obtain a near-maximum speed that you can control for an efficient takeoff into the hop. As in the long jump, you should be accelerating into the last four strides. Sprint technique is a key factor as you sprint down the runway, and acceleration is crucial to both successful hopping and speed through the jumps.

To accelerate well, you need to sprint, using strong arm action into the last four steps, which have been preceded by a solid, evenly paced run. As in the long jump, you must have a starting point for your run, followed by a second check mark. If you are starting 100 feet from the takeoff board, and if your right leg is your hopping leg, place a second check mark on the second step of your right foot (have your coach help you). That mark should be 10 to 11 feet from your starting point, and your right foot should hit the mark every time.

Try to keep increasing the length of your approach run until you are at 17 to 19 strides. Keep your approach under control, and hit the board under control and with good speed. When you hit the board, you should be up tall, and be able to continue sprinting off the board and into the hop phase.

The Takeoff

In all three phases of the triple jump, a double-arm lift is used at the instant of takeoff. This means bringing your arms back in a gathering motion and thrusting them forward and up strongly to shoulder height at the moment of takeoff. Don't lift your arms too high; your hands should stop at about chin level and your arms should be slightly flexed. Since you must carry your forward speed through three successive takeoffs, each landing should be quick, and the trajectory of the first two phases should be low so as not to convert your momentum into upward momentum.

The Hop

As you take off, the hopping (right) leg thrusts forward and upward in a circular motion, and the right thigh is at least parallel to the ground while you are in flight. Do not jump up as high you would in the long jump; instead, keep your hop somewhat low to maintain good horizontal speed into the next phase. Keep your upper body slightly forward, and your left (lower) leg relaxed and pulled close to your right leg. Concentrate on rotating—rolling—your right leg through the takeoff (that is, bringing the heel of your right foot up close to the buttock by moving your leg in a circular motion), and prepare to reach for the hop onto the right leg upon landing.

One way to practice the Hop is to hop on the grass. You can perform hopping drills, hopping on your right leg 6 to 8 times, then hopping on your left. Practice hopping on a flat foot. This is most important because it ensures that the landing leg is flexed, allowing you to stretch into the Step or Jump phase. If you land on the ball of the foot, your balance will be off and you'll have a tendency to hurry the next movement as your center of gravity moves too far over the driving leg for you to control it.

Once you're in the air after using the double-arm takeoff, think immediately about thrusting your arms back and down. The more forceful you can make this movement, the better your landing will be—you'll be able to start the up-swinging movement into the Step as soon as your right foot touches the ground.

Another useful drill is to walk on the grass and then go through a series of hops off alternating legs, rotating the legs, as described a moment ago, through each hopping motion. Concentrate on generating rhythm and power as you go into each hop.

The Step

One of the biggest factors in success as a triple jumper is to make a good Step. Most high school athletes learning the triple jump have a common problem: their Step is too short. If we broke down a 44-foot triple jump into its component parts, good measurements for each phase might look like this:

Hop:	16 feet
Step:	13 feet
Jump:	15 feet
Total	44 feet

Those numbers are general, but they should give you some idea of the relative length of the parts. By contrast, a beginner's jump might look like this:

Hop:	17 feet
Step:	11 feet
Jump:	14 feet
Total	42 feet

As the lengths suggest, if you take too long a Hop, you'll end up losing distance in the Step, which in turn causes you to slow down, reducing the distance of the Jump. Using the beginner's figures above, you would have to cover nearly 16 feet on the Jump in order to go 44 feet overall. The aim of the Step, then, is to carry the horizontal running speed left from the Hop into the Jump, and you can't do that if the Hop is too long and the Step too short. Ultimately, you want to spread that running speed as equally as you can, without wasting it, over each phase. It is nearly impossible to make the phases exactly equal, and some theories hold that the ratio should be about 35:30:35. For example, in a 50-foot triple jump, the Hop should be 17 feet 6 inches, the Step 15 feet, and the Jump 17 feet 6 inches. Again, most bad jumps are the result of too short a Step. Work on drills in which you try to "listen" to the rhythm of the three phases. What you want to feel is something like "Hop-two-three, Step-two-three, Jump-two-three." What you want to avoid is "Hop-two-three, Step, Jump-two-three."

As you go into the Step, bring your arms forward forcefully, slightly higher than in the Hop. After the hopping leg hits the ground, whip it forward, knee first, with the thigh held high. Keep your left knee high also, as this will help delay the landing into the Jump. Keep your torso straight and lean slightly forward, preparing for the landing.

As your left foot starts to come down into the Jump position, it should be sweeping backward. Thus, you mustn't step too far forward onto your left foot lest you "put on the brakes." Nor should you step down too soon, as your body will pass over the left foot too fast and not be able to generate enough overall power for the Jump. What you're striving for is an "active Step" onto the left—one moving down and back. Stepping this way will help you get off a great Jump.

You may find the Step phase of the triple jump the most difficult to learn. When learning the event, try to keep the Step phase short—under 12 feet. This will help you maintain speed as you move into the Jump phase.

The Jump

As in the long jump, this is the phase in which you should be aiming for height as well as distance. The flight and landing are the same as in the long jump, with an emphasis on maintaining good balance and keeping your feet up until the last moment. Your first two movements were performed so that you could have speed going into the Jump. If you have decent speed left after the Step phase, you'll be able to attain good height, distance, and a good landing position.

As you start to lift off the runway into the Jump, thrust both arms up as high as you can reach. By reaching up high, you will be able to slow down your forward rotation into the pit. I recommend you use the Hang technique for your legs, in which you lift your arms up and slightly behind your shoulders, and your legs trail behind you after you've jumped. Your back should be arched and your head tipped slightly back.

As you go into the landing, forcefully sweep your arms forward and down past your knees, and go for a long extension of your legs. You should land in the pit just as you would when long-jumping, with your hands behind you as your feet break the sand in front of you.

COMMON PROBLEMS IN THE TRIPLE JUMP

• Your approach is too short; your overall jumping distance is bad. *Solution:* Lengthen your approach to a distance over which you can comfortably maintain controlled speed.

• Each phase of your jump is weak. *Solution:* Again, increase your approach distance and accelerate into the last four steps to the board.

• Your Hop phase is weak. *Solution:* Hop *out,* not up, and check your balance as you leave the takeoff board.

• Your takeoff is out of control. *Solution:* Carry less speed into the takeoff.

• Your Hop is short. *Solution:* You're probably hopping too high. Again, hop out, not up.

• Your Step is short. *Solution:* Note whether your Hop is too long. Note also whether you're lifting your knee high enough and whether you're achieving a good leg split during the flight phase of the Step.

• You are getting too much height early in the Jump, rather than nearer the landing. *Solution:* Jump up and out, aiming for maximum height through the Hang phase of the Jump.

• Your posture is poor during the Jump. *Solution:* Remember, arms up, back arched, head back, legs hanging until it's time to prepare for the landing.

DRILLS FOR THE TRIPLE JUMP

The aim of triple-jump training is to develop:

• speed for the approach,
• strength and power for the takeoff,
• strength and power for the Step and Jump, and
• technique for the approach and for execution of the Hop, Step, and Jump.

Sprint Drills

• Run fast sprint intervals on the grass or track for 30 to 50 meters. Accelerate the last several runs so that you are at full speed over the last 10 meters of each run.

• Sprint downhill, slowly accelerating to full speed over the last 10 to 15 meters.

• Do resistance intervals, with a coach or partner holding you from behind in a harness. Work for 20 to 30 meters per interval, sprinting against the resistance.

• Run with the relay and sprint teams during practice.

Putting It All Together: The Triple Jump

A   B   C   D

The hop.

Here, after making a short, smooth, steadily accelerating approach (A), the jumper gathers herself for the first phase of the triple jump, the Hop. She begins by drawing her arms out and back (B, C), then takes off from the board (not shown here) on her left foot and with

The step.

This action begins with another left-foot takeoff with a double-arm lift (H), only this time the jumper strides out powerfully with her right leg (I), draws her arms back in preparation for the Jump phase, and lands on her right foot. Her right leg is flexed as it lands, and again her arms begin their powerful upward lift (J).

H   I   J

E   F   G

a double arm-lift (D, E). Her chest and left knee drive forward while her arms draw back again in preparation for the Step phase of the event (F). She lands on her left foot with her left knee slightly flexed and her arms already starting to lift powerfully forward for the next takeoff (G).

The jump.
Now the jumper takes off on her right leg with a double-arm lift (K), aiming for height as well as distance. She brings her trailing leg alongside her lead leg, with her arms overhead in the Hang position (L), and lands the jump the same as in the long jump: her hands reaching over her feet, her thighs parallel to the ground (M).

K   L   M

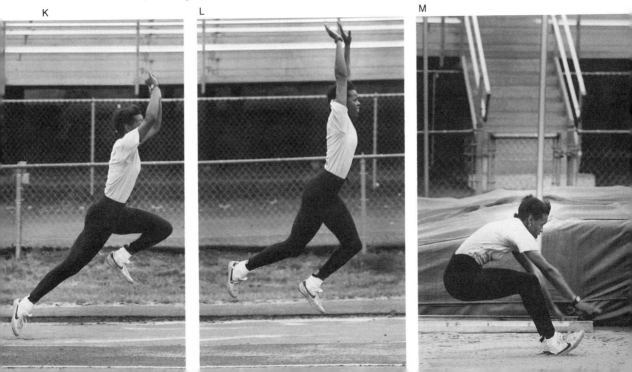

- Begin the season by hopping down the stadium stairs. Do this three times a week, working 10 to 15 minutes per session.
- Do bounding exercises on the grass (see page 22).
- Bounding drills—5 bounds per leg for distance.
- Hopping drills off each leg for strength and distance.
- Take short approach runs of 30 to 35 feet and go for a fast takeoff Hop into the sand. (Jumping into sand puts less stress on your landing foot.) Check your technique and distance.
- Set up towels at 12-foot intervals next to the runway. Work at hopping from one towel to the next, and then into the pit. Increase the distances by 6 inches every 3 weeks.
- Set up a gymnastics springboard at the end of the runway. Take a run of 25 to 35 feet, step on the board with your takeoff foot, and jump into the air, working on body position and landing in the pit.
- Mark a takeoff point 25 feet back from the edge of the pit. Using a 3-step approach, hit the takeoff mark and then go into the triple jump, landing in the pit. Repeat 8 to 10 times. Every 2 weeks, add 2 more steps to the approach, until you are up to a 7-step approach. Work on all phases of the jump.
- Do plyometric box drills (see page 27).
- Practice a full-length approach and power takeoff, working only on your Step and takeoff positions. Land in the sand. Repeat 3 or 4 times.
- Hop up stadium stairs on both feet. Work on quick movements.

Triple jumping is a difficult event, and injury can come just by practicing too hard and not letting your muscles rest. When you work out, work out fresh, not tired. Keep your muscles in good tone in order to support your weight during the bounding, hopping, and jumping exercises. A good strength training program in the weight room is a must prior to embarking on any jumping program, as you really need to develop strength before you go into any bounding or plyometric exercises. Remember, build your strength base first, then develop your jumping base for a better performance level.

THINGS TO THINK ABOUT

When you are triple-jumping, try to focus your thoughts on each phase of the jump. Here are some suggestions that might make you go just a little farther on each jump.

- Think about accelerating to the board and keeping your speed up.
- Think of the Hop as an extension of your approach.
- Go for a good wide split between the thighs at each takeoff, and lead with the knee rather than the foot.
- Think about being strong and fast with your arms and legs.
- Think about going for a big jump in the Jump phase, and for a good landing position.
- Wait for a tail wind if time permits.
- Sprint into your takeoff.

COACHING TIPS FOR THE TRIPLE JUMP

- Make sure the jumper uses a good approach and run of 17 to 21 strides.
- Make sure he starts his approach slowly and accelerates smoothly down the runway.
- The last five steps should be the jumper's fastest. Work on approaching the board aggressively.
- Watch the jumper's takeoff. His back should be straight; he should not be leaning into the Hop.
- The Hop should be low, not high into the air.
- Urge the jumper to be aggressive into the Step phase. He should drive his stepping knee to a 90-degree angle (level with his hip).
- Emphasize forceful arm action. The jumper should reach back in order to get a driving forward lift from the arms.
- Watch the Step phase closely. The jumper's posture should be erect.
- In the Jump phase, make sure the jumper uses a quick step and drives upward like a long jumper.
- At the landing, does the jumper use a big downward sweep of the arms past the legs as the feet touch down in the sand?
- Suggest that your athlete wait for a tail wind if time permits.

SAMPLE TRAINING WEEKS FOR THE TRIPLE JUMP

Because the triple jump is such a complex event, it is important that you train for all phases of the jump—the approach, the Hop, the Step, and the Jump. What you do during your many weeks of training can pay off in great jumps and a terrific sense of accomplishment.

The Off-Season (October–February)

Monday

Warm-up: 20 min.
Stride 200 meters accelerating as you approach the finish: 3 times.
50-meter acceleration sprints.
Weight work, 60–80 minutes: 75–80% of maximum.

Exercise	Sets	Reps
Step-ups with weights	3	8–12
Step-ups, no weights	3	8–12
Split squats with weights	3–5	8–12
Jump squats with weights	3–5	8–12
Skip jumps with weights	3–5	8–12
Dumbbell sprints	3–5	30 sec.
Hip flexions	3	8–12
Hip extensions	3	8–12
Sit-ups	3	20–30
Leg extensions	3	8–12
Leg curls	3	8–12
Back hyperextensions	3	15
Bench presses (incline)	3–5	3–10

Cool-down: 10–12 min.

Tuesday

Warm-up: 20 min.
Bounding drills, at least 30 meters each:
    R-R-R L-L-L R-R-R L-L-L

Hopping drills:
    R-R-R-R-R-R-R
    L-L-L-L-L-L-L

Triple-jump drills:
    R-R-L-R-R-L-R-R-L-R-R-L
    L-L-R-L-L-R-L-L-R-L-L-R

Double-leg hops: 30 meters, 5 times.
Stride 100 meters: 5 times.
Cool-down: 10–12 min.

Wednesday

Warm-up: 20 min.
Upper body plyometrics: 15 min.
Weight work: 40 min.
Film analysis with coach and teammates: 20 min.
Stretch: 10 min.
Cool-down: 10–12 min.

Thursday

Warm-up: 20 min.
Stride 50 meters, accelerating: 5 times.
Double leg vertical jumps: 15–20 times.
Double leg hopping: 30 meters, 5 times.
Hurdle hops, 10 hurdles: 8–10 times.
Hopping in the sand: 15–20 feet, 8–10 times.
Hopping down stairs: 10–12 stairs, 20 min.
Skipping: 100 meters, 5 times.
Cool-down: 10–12 min.

Friday

Warm-up: 20 min.
Weight work: 50–60 min.
Upper body plyometrics with Plyoball: 15–20 min.
Jog: 15 min.
Cool-down: 10–12 min.

Pre-Season (March)

Monday

Warm-up: 20 min.
Stride 50 meters, accelerating: 3 times.
Establish 9-step approach and run through: 8–10 times.

Take short approach steps (7 strides) and work on takeoff landing in the sand, or work off the grass. Work only on the short takeoff, not the hop: 15 min.

Short triple-jump steps (R-R-L) into pit: 15 min., L-L-R: 10 min.

Triple-jump steps off grass into pit, working on technique: 15 min.

Cool-down: 10–12 min.

Tuesday

Warm-up: 20 min.

Runway work with approach speed to takeoff board: 10 min.

Short triple jumps into pit from grass. Work only on technique: 15 min.

Weight work (follow Monday off-season schedule).

Cool-down: 10–12 min.

Wednesday

Warm-up: 20 min.

Work with 4 × 100-meter relay team.

Upper body plyometrics with Plyoball: 30 min.

Cool-down: 10–12 min.

Thursday

Warm-up: 20 min.

Box drills for plyometrics: 20 min.

Bounding and hopping drills: 30–40 meters, 5 times.

50-meter acceleration sprints: 5 times

Dumbbell weight sprints. Use light weights. Sprint short distances (20–25 meters: 5 times.

Downhill strides. Find moderate downhill, 40–60 meters long. Take long downhill strides: 5–6 times.

Cool-down: 10–12 min.

Friday

Warm-up: 20 min.

Weight work: 50–60 min.

Film analysis with coach and teammates: 20 min.

Stretching: 10 min.

Cool-down: 10–12 min.

Warm-up: 20 min.
50-meter sprints: 5–7 times, 20 min.
Triple-jump for distance: 4–6 jumps.
Long-jump off short approach: 5–8 times.
Jog: 1 mile.
Stretching: 10 min.
Cool-down: 10–12 min.

Competitive Season (April-June)

Monday

Warm-up: 20 min.
Long-jump work, short run, working on jump and landing. 15 min.
6-step approach run, then triple jump for distance, working only on technique:
   15 min.
Sprint work:
   100 meters, 3 times.
   75 meters, 3 times.
   50 meters, 3 times.
Cool-down: 10–12 min.

Tuesday

Warm-up: 20 min.
Weight work: 60 min.
   Step-ups with weights, 10 times.
   Jump squats with weight: 15–20 times.
   Dumbbell sprints: 5–6 min.
   Split squats with weights, 10 times.
   Skip jumps: 10 min.
Upper body plyometrics with Plyoball: 15 min.
Stretching. 10–12 min.
Cool-down: 10–12 min.

Wednesday

Warm-up: 20 min.
Downhill sprints: 40–60 meters, 5–6 times.

As in the long jump, practicing your approach and fine-tuning your stride length are critical for the triple jump.

Relay work with the sprinters: 30 min.
Jog: 1 mile.
Cool-down: 10–12 min.

Thursday

Warm-up: 20 min.
Weight work: 60 min.
Film analysis with coach and teammates: 20 min.
Stretching. 10–12 min.
Cool-down: 10–12 min.

Friday

Warm-up and stretching: 30 min. (Day of light rest and movement.)

Saturday

Competition day. Check run-through for good speed to the board.

7

Competing in the Jumps

Being in top physical condition, possessing solid technical skills, working with a good coach, having access to a quality jumping facility—all of these help you become a decent jumper or vaulter. However, your greatest asset in competition is what I call the competitive edge: how you think, act, and respond under competitive pressure.

Often you'll hear coaches talk about how "mentally tough" an athlete is, or how he's a "great competitor" or "a winner." All these words give you the feeling that when you compete against that person, you're up against a great athlete. And yet, athletically he may be no more gifted than anyone he's competing against. What's the difference between him and the others? In a word: *attitude.*

Are people born with this attitude of mental toughness? I think not. I believe you have to develop it as you grow into your sport. The older you get, the more mature you become, the more seasoned you become as a jumper, the greater the opportunity to develop competitive grit. Your ability to handle this pressure will improve with time—and often with help from your coach, parents, and track teammates. But as you go into competition, note how your mind is working and do all that you can to control it to your advantage.

Let's say, for example, that you're in competition as a high jumper. The bar is at your lifetime best and it is your last attempt at that height for first place. If you clear it, your team wins the conference championship. If you don't . . . well, there's always next year.

How do you handle this situation? Do you know, with every fiber of your being, that you can clear this height? Do you like being in this position, with everything riding on your shoulders?

Or do you feel like shrinking from the challenge and find yourself thinking

151

Being able to jump well in competition requires mental as well as physical preparation.

about the long ride home after you miss? Do you wonder what you'll tell your parents? Do you worry about how school will be next Monday, when everyone discusses the great chance you blew?

All pole vaulters and high jumpers can relate to these "third attempt" feelings. Unlike the long jump or triple jump, where an athlete has three to six attempts to improve in, the high jumper and pole vaulter have only three for each height. If they don't clear the bar, they're finished. The psychological demands on the high jumper and pole vaulter are unique also. You actually compete against the height at the bar, and not necessarily against other jumpers.

Pole vaulting and high jumping require that you jump better and higher as the bar is raised. Even after you've won (when all other competitors have failed at a height you've attained), you usually keep going for a greater height, only stopping after you've missed three consecutive jumps.

As a vaulter or high jumper, you should train to be in competition with the bar, not with other athletes. After all, other jumpers don't beat you—the bar beats you. Good competitors actually help you by providing stiff competition, which in turn helps you improve your performance. Ultimately, though, other jumpers should not affect you; only what you think and do in response to the height of the bar should affect you.

THE HIGH JUMPER AND POLE VAULTER

If you're a high jumper or pole vaulter in competition, here are some questions you might want to ask yourself:

- What is the wind like? Is it in my favor? How can I use the wind?
- Where is the sun?
- What is the background behind the bar like? Is it open, or are there distractions?
- Is the crowd moving around a lot?
- Is the running surface or jumping apron in good condition?
- Will the apron hold me on my plant?
- What happens if that rain starts?
- Is my vaulting pole too soft?
- Do I need to increase the length of my approach today?
- Should I change poles today—maybe try a heavier one?

- The pit seems small. Should I make some adjustments?
- The other jumpers sure look good today. How do I feel?
- Am I warming up properly?

These are just a few of the questions that can arise, and the only person who can answer them is you. I think you'll find that most jumpers in your event ask the same questions. The real question is, who can be most positive about the circumstances he faces and transform that positive attitude into a successful jump? You, or the others? Keep in mind that only you can create the proper mental attitude for success.

THE LONG JUMPER AND TRIPLE JUMPER

Knowing that you have three preliminary jumps, and if you are successful, three more jumps in the finals, means that your attitude is different from a vertical jumper's. As a horizontal jumper, you must jump against yourself for improvement and against the other jumpers in order to win.

How do you react when an opponent gets off a great jump on her first attempt? Do you look forward to the challenge, or do you find yourself settling for second or third place? Do you fall apart trying to outdo all your opponents? Or do you settle yourself down and generate a positive attitude so that you can get off a good technical jump?

If this is your last attempt and you have to improve by only 1 inch in order to win the event, do you go all out or do you play it somewhat safe, extending yourself only enough to get that last necessary inch? There are many ways that jumpers can respond to competition; the challenge for you is to bring out your best no matter what the circumstances.

Let's look at your first attempt as a horizontal jumper. Whether it's the long or the triple jump, the situation you face on the first attempt is the same. First of all, compete only against yourself on the first jump. Go for a big jump on your first attempt. Hold nothing back. If your first jump is mediocre, your opponents will be gleeful, knowing that on their first attempts they can bury you. Don't give them that satisfaction. Go for it on your first jump. Go for it on your second jump. And if you are still not doing well, or are simply holding your own in the competition, continue to go for every jump that you have coming to you. In 1984 Carl Lewis won the Olympic gold medal in the long jump on his second attempt. In 1968 Bob Beamon won the Olympic gold medal and set a world record (29 feet 2 inches) in the long jump on his first attempt. What does that tell you? The best long jumpers in the world go for it on their first attempts!

For any horizontal jump, if you approach the takeoff board with anything less than your normal jumping speed, you'll find you'll be taking off behind the board. If you approach the board at full speed but then settle into a conservative last four strides (slowing down a bit), you will be over the takeoff board and will foul the jump. Do you practice slow approaches? I think not.

If you are a triple jumper, you have to maintain a strong positive attitude toward all three phases—Hop, Step, and Jump. Do not let yourself break down just because you don't feel right once you hop, as this could lead to an injury. Remain strong, so that your legs and body position are ready for the landing and the Step phase. If your Hop is really bad, bail out; don't risk an injury. Simply run through the Step phase and come back strong on your next attempt.

When it comes to your last attempt, if you find that you need a great jump in order to score or to win that medal you've always dreamed about, think positive. Think how fast you are; what a good takeoff position you're going to establish; how good hanging in the air will feel; how long your extension will be when you hold nothing back. Visualize that great last attempt—then make it!

One of the most important suggestions I can offer to any jumper—vertical or horizontal—is to work within yourself during competition, and to spend little time visiting with other athletes. Concentrate on the challenge you face. Do not let others distract you from the event. Of course you should be courteous to others, offering help if they ask; but otherwise you should stay within yourself, keeping your mind on the event and what you have to do. Warm up properly before each attempt, get yourself ready for that moment when you are called to compete, and then go for it with all you have, every time. Hold nothing back, and enjoy your event and the pleasure of a long, successful afternoon.

THE THROWS

by Ken Shannon

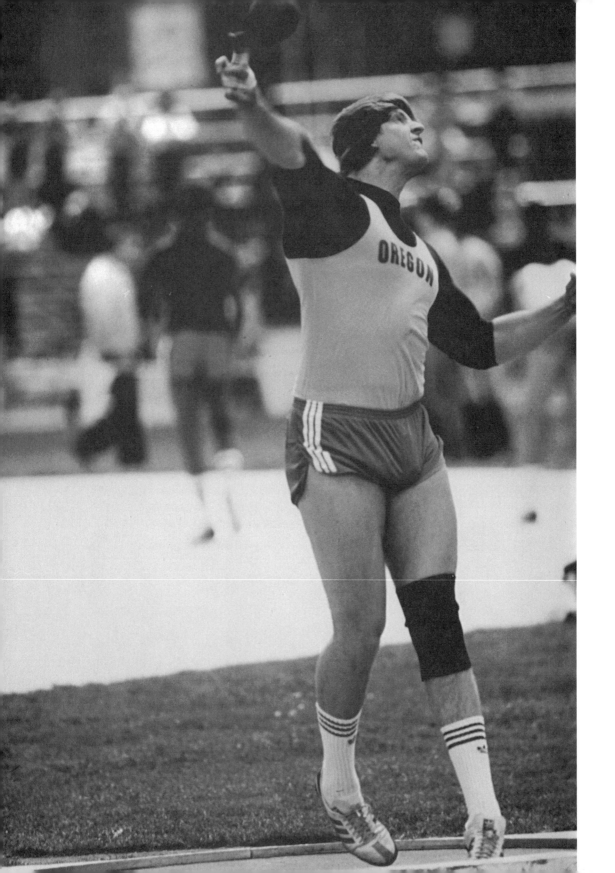

8

The Fundamentals of Throwing

I suppose someone has been trying to figure out how to throw implements like the shot put, discus, javelin, and hammer since the dawn of man. But in those prehistoric times, man's (or woman's) main concerns were accuracy and efficiency: they were trying to survive. As to how their throwing implements developed into the competitive tools we know today, I will leave that to the readers' imagination. We can safely assume that the shot put and javelin evolved from rocks and pointed limbs. Then perhaps someone got the bright idea that he could inflict greater damage on a foe by throwing a flat rock sidearm (the first discus) or by securing a heavier rock to a vine, whirling it around his head, and letting it go (the first hammer). However these throwing implements evolved, no one gave much consideration to technique until we began competing against one another. The zenith of early competitions was the ancient Olympic Games, held every four years by the Greeks from at least 776 B.C. until A.D. 393, when they were banned by Emperor Theodosius. Those early competitions helped refine track-and-field technique. As a modern-day Olympic coach, I can report that we've come a long way since the ancient Greeks and that further refinements are still underway.

It's amazing to consider how far the modern throwing events have evolved since the days of the ancient Olympic Games. And yet, one underlying factor that has kept coach and athlete transfixed from the very beginning is the excitement, the exhilaration, yes, the rapture, of seeing or making a great throw. As a thrower, you dream, you imagine, you work, sometimes for years on end, and then it happens—a great throw! It might have been far less than a school

157

Confidence, aggressiveness, a willingness to work hard and be a student of the event—these are just some of the traits you need in order to be a successful thrower.

record, but, oh man, did it feel good! Then you try, and try again, and sometimes you might be lucky enough to be able to compete against the best.

Throwers come in all shapes and sizes. It's the desire and the commitment to work hard that separate the great ones from the rest. It is true that throwers are generally big people, but there are physical tests (which we'll discuss later) that can determine a prospective thrower's innate qualities of quickness and strength. If you're a coach, knowing your athlete's emotional as well as physical capabilities is a key to nurturing his individual talents to the utmost.

Before we consider the basic mechanics of each throwing event, let's examine the psychological and physiological traits that generally help make good throwers. Over the years I've witnessed changes in coaching emphasis, both nationally and internationally. The changes have included a concern for sufficient mental toughness, a realization that weight training will not make you muscle-bound, a deep interest in biomechanical principles and sports medicine, and a host of new developments in sports psychology. The need for the latter became all too evident to me at the 1984 Olympic Games, as I watched our athletes try to respond—sometimes successfully, sometimes not—to some of the toughest emotional tests they have ever faced.

PSYCHOLOGICAL CONSIDERATIONS IN THROWING

Confidence

What a coach looks for in a prospective thrower is a confident, aggressive, hardworking, inquisitive, yet coachable young athlete. No matter what level— junior high, high school, college, elite—this is what we coaches want. I firmly believe that the successful coaching of such athletes starts in day-to-day practice, with the coach fully involved and interacting with his charges. If you assign a workout, you have to "get dirty" with your athletes, feel what they feel, be involved in all aspects of their throwing—and more.

A coach can help develop confidence in a thrower by setting proper goals, both short- and long-term. By being realistic and flexible, the desired goals can become achievable plans, and your young students will become more confident in you and in themselves.

Aggressiveness

One of the innate qualities a thrower must possess is aggressiveness. For some it is a natural trait; in others it must be developed through nurturing their self-confidence and helping them attain their goals. Coach and athlete should understand that a positive sense of aggressiveness can be attained not only from workouts but also from success in schoolwork, in competitions, and in life itself. Coach, you have to become involved in this young person's life. And you, young athlete, you have to be honest with yourself and your coach about what your priorities are and how you're tackling them. I can remember many instances in my coaching career, both at UCLA and here at the University of Washington, when athletic and academic success was achieved when an athlete ordered his priorities—academics first, athletics second—and then went after both with a passionate aggressiveness.

A Willingness to Work Hard

Hard work habits come from success and from a coach who sets a good example. Help the athletes feel they have succeeded not just when they won but when they had the courage to try! So many youngsters feel they have to win, and driven by the fear of failure, they miss the richness of experience derived from just trying. We all learn from both success and failure. The point isn't winning or losing; it's having done our best with all we have.

Other Traits

I've always felt that an athlete must be a student of his or her event. The coach must allow the athlete to be inquisitive, so that he or she can better understand why the throw "felt" the way it did. All too often the feeling of a throw is all the athlete can rely on in order to make corrections and improvements.

Practicing visual imagery (being able to mentally see oneself complete a perfect throw) is a crucial coaching aid and one that we relied upon heavily in preparing for the 1984 Olympic Games. We even took it to the point where we created mental pictures of traveling to the meet in the team bus, of what the assembly area for the athletes was like, of warming up in the Coliseum, of throwing before a crowd of 100,000. What is important here is that the athlete must feel what the total experience of a given throwing situation will be, through its entirety, and be mentally prepared for the potential distractions and pressures of competing in a crowded, emotionally charged setting.

Finally, emotional control through mental preparation for competition should be developed extensively. If you're a thrower, controlling your emotions for release at the proper time can be developed by rehearsing a set pattern or routine before competition. The value of a routine is that it gives you a set of procedures to follow the day of competition, which can be used at home or away meets. A routine is like a security blanket. It helps to eliminate any unwanted surprises, emotional or psychological. Examples of a routine might include eating a specific pre-meet meal at a certain time before competition, mentally rehearsing your warm-up and competition throws, listening to a particular piece of music, taking time to relax, going through a specific stretching routine, and so on.

PHYSIOLOGICAL CONSIDERATIONS IN THROWING

When it comes to physiology, good throwers concern themselves with body size and composition—which translates into the ratio of fat to muscle, or fat to strength. One of the concepts we will discuss later is the importance of the release speed of the throwing implement. The ability of the athlete to generate good release speed is somewhat predetermined by genetic factors—each individual is born with inherent limits of strength, speed, and endurance. But most important, if the individual is high in muscular strength and low in body fat, his or her chances of performing successfully are greatly increased. You cannot move fat explosively, either vertically or horizontally, whether you're trying to run, jump, or throw. Your body-fat level has to be low in order for you to throw well—in men, ideally 8 to 10 percent; in women 12 to 15 percent. That means that if your body-fat percentages are significantly higher, you have to start looking at what you eat (more on this later) and getting in shape.

I am a firm believer in consistent, well-planned, and well-organized practices involving controlled amounts of hard work. But I also know that if the body is to respond successfully to the stress of exercise, there must be an adaptation, or recovery, phase—a period of planned rest—as well. Athletes and coaches both should remember that if stress is too frequent or too intense, the body cannot adapt and will literally break down. The result is an injured athlete and possibly a ruined throwing career.

The *volume* of training applies to the amount of weight lifted in weight training and to the number of drills and throws allowed in practice. These volumes should not be exceeded until the athlete has reached an appropriate level of conditioning.

Specificity of training refers to those exercises and drills that are of specific benefit to the thrower. For example: throwing requires strength and quickness, so having a discus thrower run 5 miles a day as a part of training is futile. Short sprints are great and aid in developing explosive quickness, but running distances of a mile or more are actually a hindrance.

The *intensity* with which you perform an exercise depends largely upon your fitness and is a highly individual matter. I believe intensity originates from the ability to concentrate, and that both intensity and concentration can remain high with adequate recovery time between exercises and workouts. You cannot be consistently intense if you rush through a workout—which leads to the next principle.

The *frequency* and *duration* of a workout must match your capabilities as an athlete. The old saying "More is not always better" simply means that back-to-back hard days are not always advisable. Rather, at some time during the season, your workout schedule should be individualized and perhaps lightened to allow your body adequate time to recover after intensive workouts.

THE BASIC MECHANICS OF THE THROWS

A scientific approach to coaching is essential in helping us understand and apply basic laws of physics to our athletes. The real key, I think, is in knowing when and how to apply these physical laws to each individual. But watch out: don't make it complicated, either for yourself or for the athlete. I like the old k.i.s.s. principle—"Keep it simple, stupid"—because a coach can often bog a young star down with complicated scientific jargon when the star is only capable of understanding how a good throw feels.

Basically there are only three or four factors that contribute to a successful throw:

1. *Speed of release.* This is the most important factor and refers to how fast the implement leaves the hand.

2. *Angle of release.* This differs in each throw and is determined by body position and the height of the implement at release.

3. *Height of release* also differs in each throw. This is determined by measuring from the point of release to the ground.

4. *The effects of air resistance.* In the case of the javelin and the discus, an aiding wind can greatly increase the distance of the throw.

A number of other factors are pertinent to the throws:

Motion. Motion implies a continuous change of position, both linear (straight line) and rotary (circular).

Axis indicates the point around which rotary motion occurs.

Rotary motion indicates the turning motion of an object around an axis. The object might be a hammer, and the axis a hammer thrower; a discus, with the axis being the discus thrower; or the shot, with the axis being the rotation shot-putter.

Linear motion indicates movement along a straight line, such as the path of a javelin thrower or a conventional shot-putter.

Velocity refers to the distance traveled in a specific direction, measured by time. An example would be the speed imparted to any of the four throwing implements at its point of release.

Acceleration simply means an increase in velocity or a positive rate of change (faster).

Deceleration indicates a slowing down of velocity or a negative rate of change (slower). Often referred to as "blocking" with the body at the finish of the four throws.

Horizontal velocity indicates speed moving forward.

Vertical velocity indicates movement straight up or down.

Force means any physical change that can modify the nature of the body. In *Track and Field Techniques Through Dynamics,* Tom Ecker mentions the force the shot-putter exerts against the shot and the force of the discus thrower's foot upon impact in the middle of the circle.

Ground reaction is the amount of force returned from the ground, and it is equal to the force applied. In the case of the discus thrower's foot making contact in the circle, the greater the force against the circle, the greater the lift.

Center of mass is the point in an object or a body at which its mass can be considered to be centered. This point is not constant in human bodies; it changes as the body's segments move during athletic activity.

Transferring momentum occurs when one part of the body takes up the momentum of another part of the body. For example, when a javelin thrower blocks (decelerates the body) during the last step of a throw, the momentum of the lower body is transferred to the upper body and arm as the throw is made.

Inertia means the body's resistance to change in motion. For instance, in the hammer throw, once the rotary motion begins around the longitudinal axis, the body's rotational inertia tends to cause the body to continue to rotate.*

Some unique considerations in the application of the biomechanical principles in the four throwing events can result in some critical and astounding results:†

In the shot put, one of the things we will discuss will be converting horizontal and rotary force into vertical force. If the thrower could improve the horizontal and rotary forces behind his throw and thereby increase the speed of his release by 10 percent, his throwing distance would improve 21 percent! In the same way, height of release can be improved by enhancing ground reaction (more energy returned to the shot put) and by an increase in the strength and size of the athlete. If one were able to raise the height of release just 6 to 12 inches, the improvement in distance could be as much as 12 inches.

The optimum angle for the shot is 40 to 42 degrees (this will vary somewhat with each thrower). To achieve that throwing angle, you must work to increase the vertical velocity of your throw. As we will see, this is done by using the legs and trunk effectively—*not the arm*—and by transferring the force they generate to the throw itself.

In the discus, the release angle is 34 to 40 degrees. The lower angle reflects a need for greater horizontal velocity (speed of release) in the throw, and a respect for the effects of air resistance (wind direction) during the throw. Great discus throwers are able to manipulate the amount of horizontal and vertical velocity of the throw according to wind variations. Using the wind effectively can result in up to a 10-foot improvement in the throw.

In the hammer and javelin, an improvement in the speed of release can be very dramatic. The optimum angle of release for the hammer is 42 to 44 degrees, and for the javelin (because of the new physical changes to the implement itself) about 30 to 35 degrees. A 10 percent increase in speed for the hammer release can result in a 40-foot improvement. Maintaining a 3-inch-longer radius while performing the turns in the hammer (radius defined here as the distance between the vertical axis—the thrower—and the hammer head) could improve a throw by 18 feet!

---

*Ecker, Tom. *Track and Field Techniques Through Dynamics,* pages 15–18.
†Tom Ecker's *Track and Field Techniques* (above) is the source of the statistical information in this discussion.

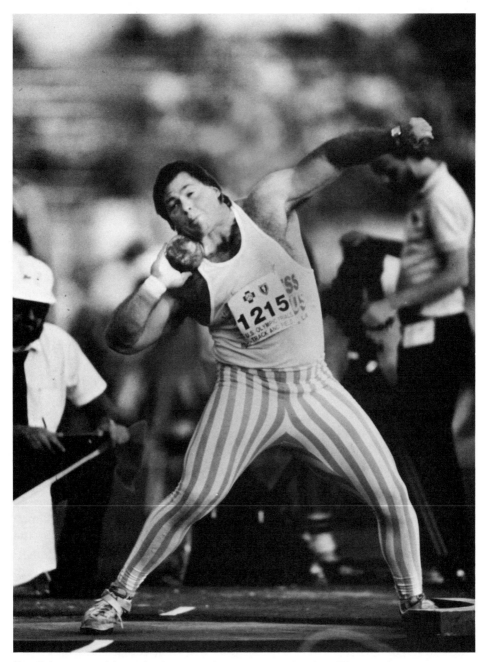

Practicing proper biomechanics as a thrower can make the difference between a great throw and a mediocre one.

The javelin presents a real challenge because of the drastic implement changes. In 1985 the IAAF changed the physical characteristics of the javelin to keep the implement from traveling as far while in flight. However, speed of release and air resistance remain primary concerns.

If you're going to throw successfully or coach successfully, you need to have at least a basic grasp of these biomechanical concepts. They can help you make numerous refinements in your technique. More important, they can help you throw better and farther.

9

Training for the Throws

What does a thrower need to be successful? We have already discussed the importance of desire and hard work. What are the basic physical qualities you need, assuming you are persistent, hardworking, and tenacious?

First of all, you don't have to be 6 feet 5 and weigh 250 pounds in order to throw far! Being tall and weighing a lot obviously can help, but as I said earlier, good throwers come in all shapes and sizes. I would love, for instance, to be able to take all the NFL middle linebackers and make hammer throwers of them, or take all the NBA centers and make them discus throwers, or take the NFL centers and pulling guards and train them for the shot put, and as for the javelin—well, let me have the quarterbacks! These are great body types and most assuredly typify those of Olympic-caliber athletes. But I have seen 5-foot 10-inch, 225-pound athletes throw the 16-pound shot over 62 feet, and I have seen 5-foot 10-inch, 185-pound javelin throwers throw over 260 feet and become NCAA champions. So let's not prevent the so-called little guy from trying, but note instead that *all* these people possess certain basic physical qualities:

Hand strength. The size of the hand is not crucial, but strength is. Forearm and wrist strength both contribute to hand strength. Hand strength allows the athlete to better control the implement, all the way to the moment he releases it. How do you determine hand strength? There are many tests, I suppose, but I like to use the simple old handshake. Have you ever experienced a "limp fish" handshake? Rarely does that person turn out to be a good thrower. By contrast, the athletes I have coached who became good throwers had all performed hard manual labor at one time or another. They developed hand strength through using a shovel, ax, pick, or manure fork—even a gill net or a chain saw! Now, before you city folks go out and start tearing the block down, be assured that

167

Strength training is at the heart of any thrower's training program.

you can also develop hand strength by doing Olympic lifts and dead lifts with weights—exercises that we'll demonstrate later.

Innate quickness. Does quickness mean that you can catch a fly in flight between your index finger and thumb? No. It means having quick feet and explosive leg strength. Once again, Olympic lifting and squats can help you develop your quickness, so don't feel you haven't a chance if you're somewhat slow.

Innate basic strength. Quickness and strength go together—you have to have innate basic strength to be quick. A youngster who has worked hard and is not afraid to sweat has basic strength. Other coaches have told me that they use the dead lift exercise as an indicator of basic strength; I would also add the bench press.

Aggressiveness. You don't have to be a street fighter to be a competitor, but you must be aggressive by nature—especially when you are on the runway or in the throwing ring. This is a tough attribute to determine in some people, so I do not think you can eliminate the "nice guys" at first glance. For most people, competitive aggressiveness develops from having confidence in their ability and in themselves. Such confidence can easily and properly carry over into life itself, which is one of the main reasons competitive athletics is so important to youngsters. Throwers can come from other sports—football (obviously), baseball, tennis, soccer, and so on—but you do not have to be a pugnacious defensive or offensive tackle to be a successful thrower.

TRAINING PROGRAMS

Let's say you are an eighth-grader or a high school freshman interested in going out for track and field, the throws in particular, but you are not sure how to begin. Which event should you go out for? You wonder, What should I specialize in? Not so fast. There's plenty of time to specialize later. For now, I suggest you approach the sport more as a generalist. Try to sample all the throwing events and get a feel for the one you like the most and are good at.

Testing for Innate Athletic Ability

Under the supervision of a qualified coach or physical education instructor, you should take a series of preliminary tests to help determine your innate athletic ability.

The following seven tests are suggested as a means to discovering the physical qualities we have discussed. We also use these exercises here at the University of Washington to help determine an athlete's improvement in physical fitness and strength. My good friend and colleague Dr. Ken Foreman (the 1980 and 1988 Olympic coach for women), of Seattle Pacific University, has done considerable research on this selective process for all events in track and field. I have used his information relating to the first four tests, but I have either modified, changed, or added to the weight-lifting tests he suggests. In the last three tests the weight is lifted only once.

1. Standing long jump   women 7 ft.
                              men 8 ft.

2. Vertical jump   women 18 in.
                              men 26 in.

3. Softball throw   women 190 ft.
                              men 250 ft.

4. 50-yard sprint (use a running start)   women 6.9 sec.
                              men 6.2 sec.

5. Bench press   women 95% of body weight
                              men 125% of body weight

6. Dead lift   women 115% of body weight
                              men 150% of body weight

7. Half squat   women 135% of body weight
                              men 195% of body weight

The test results shown above are good indicators of natural talent specific to the throws. But if you can't achieve these results, don't worry. With training you *can* become an excellent thrower.

The Yearly Cycle: An Overview

As a thrower, you have to consider your long-range plans first, and then be specific during different times of the year. That is, after establishing your goals for the end of the season (strength goals; throwing goals, both distance and technique; goals for the seven tests above), you work backward: When should my strength peak? What meets am I going to aim for? What drills am I going to emphasize, and for how long? A yearly cycle is necessary even for a junior- or senior-high athlete who may be involved in more than one sport. The coach must take all scheduling factors into consideration in order to establish an optimum yearly training cycle for the young thrower. And don't forget: most young athletes can peak mentally and emotionally only three to four times in a season.

To be an effective thrower takes diligent, intelligent planning and continual adjustments in your training program. Yet there has to be a master plan containing both short- and long-term goals. These goals should involve not only competitive schedules and throwing workouts, but also the level of quality from workout to workout. The workouts discussed in this chapter will be weight training for strength development; medicine ball and gymnastic exercises for general warm-up, explosiveness, flexibility, and coordination; running programs; and some basic drills that can be used as a general tune-up before practice begins. Plyometrics, described in Chapter 2, will not be discussed again here, except to mention that in the precompetitive phase they are extremely beneficial and should be incorporated into a training program for practice once a week.

Career Progress

If we were to plot the ideal progression of a thrower, it might look like this:

In junior high school or freshman and sophomore years in high school, the athlete is introduced to different events in track and field, based on the preliminary tests mentioned earlier. Several events are good for the overall development of the individual, including the hurdles, long jump, triple jump, and short sprints. In his formative years, the thrower should not specialize but rather be involved in several track-and-field events. In high school more specialization is allowed, but I encourage involvement in at least two different events.

In college some throwers can excel in more than one event, but eventually they must concentrate on one. A few weeks off to "regroup" at the end of the season is good, but a year-round training program is a must.

The open athlete (usually a college graduate who continues to compete) has a much broader fitness base because of past years of training work. The open athlete's season often lasts until late summer or early fall, which means he or she trains longer than the college athlete before the first competition and does not have as many early meets. And, given his or her experience and fitness level, once training commences the open athlete tends to concentrate on event-specific drills and exercises for throwing.

I feel it is a mistake for mature, or elite, athletes to continue to strive for more strength each season. They must be event-specific concerning strength and allow more time and energy to perfect skills, work on conditioning development (by integrating activities such as plyometrics and gymnastics into their workouts), develop the transverse and abdominal muscles for greater torso strength and add two practice workouts a day, in throwing or related activities, to their schedules.

See pages 181–183 for sample training schedules.

Strength and Power

Through modern science and by trial and error, we have discovered many and varied means by which strength is developed. The fact remains that if you are strong, you can throw the implement farther than someone less strong, because you can release it faster. Release speed remains the primary reason we work so hard to develop strength.

At the same time, there is a limit as to how much energy and time should be spent on developing strength. Just as important is the process of acquiring proper technique. If you are strong, your chances of learning and acquiring proper technique are greatly enhanced. The key to developing both strength and technique is patience. Patience involves working from a well-designed training program that allows you enough energy for both skill and strength development. In the beginning we allow more time for learning technique while we are developing a base of strength. Just as in throwing itself, there are numerous skills to be learned in the different strength exercises. I recommend that throwers develop their strength and throwing technique on a percentage basis: The junior-high athlete should devote 80 percent of her or his time to throwing and 20 percent to weight training. The high school athlete would spend 60 percent of the time throwing and 40 percent on weights. The college and open athlete's training will obviously intensify, but the emphasis for each will vary depending on the time of year.

At the University of Washington we use three types of programs during the course of the school year. The first is *foundation building,* which prepares the athlete for more mentally intensive lifting with heavier weights at a predetermined date. It's also a time for relearning basic skills in each exercise or for acquiring new skills. It's very similar to a program for someone who is undertaking weight training for the first time. The program is typified by fewer sets and more repetitions, and in some instances the rest interval between sets and exercises is controlled. Depending on the age and maturity of the individual, it is not a time for lifting heavier weights but rather a time of moderation, control, and endurance building. The length of the program is usually 3 to 4 weeks. This is also a time to do medicine ball exercises and gymnastics.

The second program becomes much more involved as time goes on, because this is where the strength development takes place. We call it the *power program,* power defined as force over distance times speed. This program usually lasts for 4 to 5 months, during which the thrower goes through 4- to 6-week cycles. At Washington we have lifting contests to determine progress, and we also employ percentages of the maximum a thrower can lift in a given exercise for the amount of weight we want lifted for each set. I have found this system to be very useful because by controlling the amount of energy expended, the coach can control the amount of weight lifted; in short, he can prevent the individual from attempting too much too soon. It is a gradual process, but one that, as we shall see, intensifies after two or three cycles. We attempt to strengthen each general area of the body by exercising it twice weekly: legs and arms; stomach and torso; back and hips. We limit the number of exercises for each session to four or six. We also throw 3 days a week during this time, and we begin plyometrics.

The third session lasts for the remainder of the season, usually 6 weeks, and we call it the *maintenance phase,* meaning that the throwers' strength has peaked for the season and they are now trying to keep the strength level up for as long as possible. There are many theories about how best to conduct this period, but the concept we have employed recently involves 2 sets of 5 repetitions for a warm-up, followed by 3 sets of 6 repetitions at 70 to 80 percent of a thrower's maximum lifting capability in a particular exercise, as fast as possible but under control. The recovery period between sets is at least 4 minutes, and we use only the basic lifts such as squat, bench press, clean, and snatch. Any exercise beyond those is a matter of individual preference. I might add that this becomes a highly individual time which can and will vary, depending on the circumstances. But the thing we are most pleased about is that the strength level remains very high and we have ample time for throwing.

A Foundation Lifting Program for Beginners

What follows is a general, all-around beginning lifting schedule. It can be completed in about 1 hour, allowing a 2-minute rest interval between sets. It should be done 3 times a week (Monday, Wednesday, Friday), starting at about 60 to 70 percent of your maximum effort. For detailed instruction on all the strength exercises discussed here, see *Sports Illustrated Strength Training* by John Garhammer (New York: Sports Illustrated Winner's Circle Books, 1987).

Warm-up Exercise: 1 set of 10 reps. This is done in one continuous movement from the ground to overhead. Allow the weight to touch the ground, but do not relax before starting back up. (Inhale going up, exhale coming down.)

Two-Hand Press: 5 sets of 5 reps. This exercise should be done with a rapid finish. Emphasize the drive at the finish with an explosive push. (Inhale from the top down, exhale at the top.)

Parallel Squats: 3 sets of 10 reps. Keep your head up and your back slightly arched. Don't go down any farther than thighs parallel to the floor. (Inhale going down, breathing high in the chest, not in the diaphragm. Exhale once again as you proceed back up. Breathe in and out forcefully, through the mouth.)

Two-Arm Pullovers: 2–3 sets of 10 reps. Lying on your back on a weight bench, back flat and feet on the floor, start with the barbell at chest level; lower it behind the head and then raise it to a position back over the chest. Do not relax as the weight nears the ground; keep the tension in the arms and start right back up. (Breathe high in the chest, not low in the diaphragm. Inhale as the weight goes toward the ground, then hold. Exhale at the top.)

Two-Arm Curls: 2–3 sets of 10 reps. Start with the arms straight, palms up. Pull or curl the hands toward the shoulder. At the bottom, straighten the arms out and relax them each time. (Inhale going up, exhale coming down.) You can also perform this exercise using an E-Z Curl bar.

Bench Press: 2–3 sets of 10 reps. Drive fast and hard on the way up. (Breathe high in the chest on the way down. Then exhale at the top.)

Toe Raises: 3 sets of 15 reps. The block should be 2½ inches thick. Raise all the way up, then touch the heels to the floor. (Breathe normally.)

Stiff-Legged Dead Lift and Shoulder Shrug: 2 sets of 10 reps. Raise the shoulders toward the ears and rotate them back as far as possible. Bend forward and touch the weight to the ground. (Inhale coming up, high in the chest. Exhale coming down.)

Side-Straddle Hop: 1 set of 100 reps. Start with your feet together. Hop sideways, from side to side, staying on your toes throughout the entire exercise. When you reach 80 reps, try to increase the speed. (Normal breathing.)

Side Bends: 1 set of 50 reps, counting each side as 1 rep. (Exhale bending down, inhale coming up.)

Upright Rowing: 2 sets of 20 reps. Start with the arms straight down. Using a narrow grip, pull the bar to the chin. (Inhale on the way up, high in the chest. Exhale coming down.)

Sit-ups: 1 set of 50 reps. Hook the toes under the bar and touch the ground on the other side of the bar. When this becomes easy, hold 10 pounds behind your head; gradually add more weight.

A Power Program for Beginners

The following training schedule is a general power program for a high school athlete on a program using one 4-week cycle before percentages are assigned as described earlier. The keys to this program are:

- Heavier weights, more sets, fewer repetitions.
- Increase weight 5 to 50 pounds or more each set.
- Four workouts per week and a test at the end of the cycle.

Monday and Thursday

Dead lift: 5 sets of 5 reps.
Cleans: 5 sets of 5 reps.
Squats: 5 sets of 5 reps.
Dumbbell flies: 5 sets of 5 reps.
Two-arm curls: 5 sets of 5 reps.

Tuesday and Friday

Seated behind-neck presses: 5 sets of 5 reps.
Bench presses: 5 sets of 5 reps.
Incline presses: 5 sets of 5 reps.
Snatches: 5 sets of 5 reps.
Leg extensions: 5 sets of 5 reps.
Leg curls: 5 sets of 5 reps.

An Advanced Lifting Program

The following is an example of a weight training program for advanced throwers, be they high school, college, or elite. This type of program should be undertaken only by the more mature athlete (sophomore, junior, senior in college, and open) who has lifted before, and it could also be undertaken by an advanced senior in high school. It is important to remember that there are no shortcuts to strength and to a low body-fat count. Time, patience, intelligent work, and planning are essential. The most important thing to remember is that you should *not* exceed the designated percentage assigned to each workout. For detailed instruction on all the strength exercises discussed here, see *Sports Illustrated Strength Training* by John Garhammer (New York: Sports Illustrated Winner's Circle Books, 1987). You and your coach must now decide what you are going to emphasize, and on what days.

Example #1   Monday, Wednesday, Friday: upper body
                Tuesday, Thursday, Saturday: lower body

Example #2   Monday and Thursday: upper body
                Tuesday and Friday: lower body

Example #3   Monday and Friday: upper body
                Tuesday, Thursday, Saturday: lower body

All of this occurs after one 3-week cycle for general fitness, such as circuit training with moderate weights 3 times a week, and a 4-week cycle of general power training, with a test the fifth week using two repetitions, not one, for each exercise tested. If you followed these two earlier programs, you are now ready to start a 4- to 6-week cycle using percentages based on the second cycle tests. Let's say your maximum lift in the bench press is 350 pounds; in the squat, 400; in the clean, 315; and in the snatch, 205. A percentage chart from which to gauge how much to lift on any given day might look like this:

Percentage	Bench Press	Squat	Clean	Snatch
100	350	400	315	205
95	330	380	300	195
90	315	360	285	185
85	300	340	270	175
80	280	320	255	165
75	265	300	240	155
70	245	280	225	145

The weight training schedule for the third and fourth cycles might look like this:

Monday and Friday

Medicine ball exercises: 10 min.
Stretching.
Warm-up drills: 15 min.
Throw: 20 times.
Weights:

Week 1   Snatches: 70%—5 reps
                            80%—3 reps
                            85%—2 sets of 3 reps
                            90%—3 sets of 1 rep

            Bench presses: 70%—5 reps
                            80%—2 sets of 5 reps
                            85%—5 reps
                            90%—5 sets of 1 rep

            Incline presses: 4 sets of 5 reps

            Flies: 4 sets of 5 reps, with dumbbells

            Seated rows: 4 sets of 5 reps

            Curls: 4 sets of 5 reps

Week 2   Snatches: 75%—5 reps
                            85%—3 sets of 3 reps
                            90%—3 sets of 1 rep

            Bench presses: 75%—5 reps
                            80%—5 reps
                            85%—2 sets of 5 reps
                            90%—5 sets of 1 rep

            Incline presses: 4 sets of 5 reps
            Flies: 4 sets of 5 reps, with dumbbells
            Seated rows: 4 sets of 5 reps
            Curls: 4 sets of 5 reps

Week 3   Snatches: 75%—5 reps
                            85%—3 sets of 3 reps
                            90%—3 sets of 1 rep

            Bench presses: 75%—5 reps
                            85%—3 sets of 5 reps
                            90%—5 sets of 1 rep

	Incline presses:	4 sets of 5 reps
	Flies:	4 sets of 5 reps, with dumbbells
	Seated rows:	4 sets of 5 reps
	Curls:	4 sets of 5 reps

Week 4	Snatches:	75%—5 reps 85%—2 sets of 3 reps 90%—3 reps 95%—3 sets of 1 rep
	Bench presses:	75%—5 reps 85%—5 reps 90%—2 sets of 5 reps 95%—5 sets of 1 rep
	Incline presses:	4 sets of 5 reps
	Flies:	4 sets of 5 reps, with dumbbells
	Seated rows:	4 sets of 5 reps
	Curls:	4 sets of 5 reps

Week 5	*Test on snatch and bench press.*

Wednesday

Gymnastics: 20 min.
Throw: 30–40 times.
Plyometrics: 20 min.

Tuesday, Thursday, and Saturday

Jog: ½ mile.
Incline sit-ups: 20 times.
Back raises: 20 times.
Side bends: 6 each side with barbell.
Twists: 6 each side with barbell.
Cleans:

Weeks 1 and 2:	70%—5 reps 75%—3 reps 80%—2 sets of 5 reps 85%—5 reps

Squats:

Weeks 1 and 2:	70%—5 reps
	75%—3 reps
	80%—2 sets of 5 reps
	85%—5 reps

Leg extensions:	4 sets of 5 reps.
Curls:	4 sets of 5 reps.
Dead lifts:	4 sets of 5 reps.

Week 5: Test on cleans and squats.

Flexibility and Coordination Training for Throwing

Strength and power are crucial in the throwing events, but equally important are flexibility and coordination. During the power phase of weight training, the thrower often tends to lose joint flexibility, becoming tight and thereby uncoordinated. As a result he also becomes prone to minor stress-related injuries.

Medicine ball (pages 29–39), gymnastics, and flexibility drills are important as a warm-up before throwing. These exercises should be performed extensively in the beginning of the season, but as time progresses, you should be able to determine which exercises you want to eliminate or maintain in your training schedule. I cannot stress this enough because these warm-up exercises tend to eliminate soreness and promote joint and tendon flexibility, especially in the early stages of weight training.

1. *Medicine ball exercises.*
2. *Gymnastics exercises:*

    Tumbling: forward and backward rolls, cartwheel to round-offs, handstands.

    Horizontal bar: swing, pullover, kip.

    Still rings: swing, skin cat, bird's nest.

3. *Flexibility drills:*

    Bounding, skipping, hopping, kar-i-o-ka. (See page 248 for a description of the kar-i-o-ka.)

    Skip forward: arms windmill backward.

    Skip backward: arms windmill backward.

Skip sideways: arms windmill backward.

Skip forward, swinging right arm across body and left knee across vertical axis.

Skip forward, swinging left arm across body and right knee across vertical axis.

Skip forward and upward, swinging arms alternately overhead—right arm swings upward as left knee lifts, etc.

4. *Running:* It is important to remember that moderate jogging (800 yards to 1 mile) and intense running (short sprints, 40 to 60 yards) should be an integral part of your weekly training schedule. I like to incorporate the jogging before weight training on days when the emphasis will be on lower-body weight work (leg days), and short sprints one or two times a week after throwing. Usually 10 sprints will suffice, with a walk-back interval. Running aids in coordination, develops explosive leg power, and can help prevent stress-related injuries.

NUTRITION AND THROWING

As you probably already recognize, as a thrower your need for energy is extreme. In addition, you must be concerned about your body-fat ratio (ideally around 10 to 12 percent) while continually trying to make gains in strength, muscle size, and body weight. Correct and efficient body mass is essential for a thrower, and there are no shortcuts. You must progress at your own rate, as your body type and overall health dictate. Overeating, an ill-planned diet, and massive doses of vitamins are not conducive to your well-being and can have serious side effects. As a general rule, your food intake must help you maintain your optimal body weight for maximum performance and must furnish the calories, amino acids, vitamins, and minerals necessary for growth, development, and function.

Carbohydrates are a major part of the caloric requirement for body growth and function. Protein and fats are second. As a general guideline, for physical training your diet should include approximately 20 percent fat, 15 percent protein, and 65 percent carbohydrates.

Vitamins serve as an essential catalyst for transforming energy and are utilized in large quantities to help meet the metabolic demands of strenuous athletic activity. Signs of vitamin deficiency include weakness, fatigue, constipation, loss of appetite, headache, disturbed sleep, irritability, depression, and inability to concentrate. Taking massive doses of vitamins, however, can lead to toxic reactions, resulting in illness or even death. Play it safe with vitamins: one multivitamin supplement a day is a sufficient catalyst for your energy needs.

Some Basic Guidelines

Here are some other considerations for planning a diet:

Breakfast should contain at least one fourth of your caloric intake for the day. Lunch should contain about one fourth of the daily caloric intake. Dinner should contain foods abundant in proteins, vitamins, and minerals.

For in-between snacks I like the following "power" formula:

> 1 quart 1 or 2 percent milk
>
> 1 packet instant breakfast mix
>
> 3 tablespoons powdered milk

Mix in a blender or shaker. Add fruit (as desired). Blend again. Drink 1 glass 3 times daily. Store mix in refrigerator.

Other between-meal snacks can include raw vegetables, granola bars, or (my old standby while traveling) peanut butter and jam sandwiches with raisins.

Beyond adequate carbohydrates in your diet, water is the single most important element for an effective, safe, nutritional program. Fluid loss can be severe when you're working out, and dehydration robs the muscles of strength and can have dire effects if the body's fluid balance is not maintained. During training you should drink more water than you think you need, as the body's thirst mechanism often misleads you into believing you've replaced enough water with a single glass. Be aware that you can lose nearly 2 quarts of water per hour during strenuous exercise in severe heat, and this fluid must be replaced. By drinking water frequently (every 20 minutes during workouts), you'll maintain your strength much longer.

If you decide to become a thrower, remember that you are taking a vow, making a pact with yourself, to train your mind and body to perform to their ultimate potential. This means you must be disciplined, you must care about what you are doing, you must love the process that will lead to your peak performance. Training isn't always easy; there can be days when you do not want to train and when you become frustrated. But if you really care about what you are doing, and if you want to find out how good you can become, you will stick to it. Make sure that you and your coach monitor your progress as you go through your training year. If any aspect of your training is not producing what you planned, modify it so that it meshes with your capabilities.

Finally, if anyone recommends anabolic steroids, or some other "wonder" drug, *don't take them.* Anabolic steroids are not only illegal, they are dangerous: potentially deadly, at the very least they can lead to permanent harmful side effects. No matter what you may hear otherwise, there can be no condoning the use of anabolic steroids by throwers or any other athletes. To repeat: *Don't take anabolic steroids!*

SAMPLE TRAINING SCHEDULE FOR HIGH SCHOOL ATHLETES

Pre-Season (March)

Monday, Wednesday, Friday

Jog 800 meters and stretch.
Medicine ball exercises.
Drills and light throwing; short sprints.

Tuesday, Thursday, Saturday

Jog 800 meters and stretch.
Gut work and weight training.
Tuesday: gymnastics, 20 min.
Saturday: plyometrics, 20 min.

Sunday

Rest.

Competitive Season (April–June)

Monday, Wednesday, Thursday

Jog 800 meters and stretch.
Drills and throw.
Short sprints.

Tuesday, Thursday, Sunday

Jog 800 meters and stretch.
Gut work and weight training (heaviest on day after competition).
One day, either plyometrics, gymnastics, or medicine ball exercises: 10 min.

Friday

Rest on day before competition.

The Off-Season (October–March)

Another sport and weight training (building a new base).

SAMPLE TRAINING SCHEDULE FOR COLLEGE ATHLETES

Early Summer

Time off for rest and relaxation.
Begin planning for the new season with coach. Discuss training schedule adjustments, technique adjustments, strength levels, and other variables.

Late Summer

Begin new strength foundation.

Fall and Winter

Peak strength no earlier than March.
Drills before throwing, and audiovisual aids for technique practice.
Plyometrics and gymnastics once a week. (Plyometrics on days when no weight training for legs is involved.)
Emphasis on torso and abdominal strength 3 days per week.
Weight training, 4 to 6 days per week.
Work on flexibility constantly.
Start throwing in late fall or early January.

Competitive Season (April–June)

Determine when strength level should peak—usually 6 to 8 weeks before the season ends.

Fewer weight training exercises, performed 4 days a week. Example:
   Monday, Wednesday: legs
   Tuesday, Thursday: upper body

Fewer drills; discontinue plyometrics 2 weeks before competition.

Concentrate more on throwing. Work for rhythm and timing; emphasize total throw by concentrating on fewer technique skills. Do not throw when frustrated.

Have throws videotaped during practice and at meets; then review those tapes. Try to determine early in week what skills you will emphasize.

The Shot Put

The shot put is probably the most aggressive of the events in track and field. Performed in a 7-foot circle with a 4-inch-high toe board at the front, where the shot is released, the event has seen the evolution of two distinct methods of throwing. The *glide* involves a linear motion across the ring; the *rotary* or *spin* involves a rotation (one turn) along a straight line.

No matter which technique you use, one of the first and hardest things to remember is the difference between "putting" and throwing. While the object of the event is to cast the weighted ball as far as possible, this must be done in a particular way. The shot should remain in contact with your neck throughout the ring crossing and be "put" or "punched" rather than thrown at the release. This means that your elbow remains behind the shot at all times. Imagine a stiff jab or punch at an opponent: the fist leads and the elbow follows. Try to keep this concept in mind throughout your practice sessions; not only is it a more effective means of getting the shot out there, it will also save wear and tear on your elbow.

Since there are different dimensions for the implement depending on your age and sex, use the shot best suited to you. As a beginner you may want to use a lighter shot than the one designated until you have strengthened the appropriate muscles.

THE IMPLEMENT

The shot is usually a solid ball of iron, steel, or brass, sometimes covered with rubber for indoor use. Dimensions are as follows:

Successfully putting the shot requires explosive power.

High school men: 12 pounds, 3⅞ to 4⅝ inches in diameter

High school women: 8 pounds, 3¾ to 4⅜ inches in diameter

Collegiate men: 16 pounds, 4⅜ to 5⅛ inches in diameter

Collegiate women: 8 pounds, 13 ounces, 3¾ to 4⅜ inches in diameter

Again, the size or weight of the shot you use depends entirely on your age. In this country, some schools use the 10-pound shot for junior-high and high school freshmen boys. However, by the time you are a sophomore or junior in high school you should be using the 12-pound shot. The transition for men from high school (12-pound) to college or open (16-pound) is tough because of the tremendous difference in weight. Some countries use the 14-pound for high school seniors, which I think makes more sense. Otherwise, if you are a 60-foot shot-putter in high school, you can expect a 5- to 7-foot decrease in your throw once you start using the 16-pound shot. To reestablish and improve on your old distance, you have to become a stronger and more efficient thrower. Concentration, persistence, and patience are traits the athlete and the coach must both have during this difficult time of change.

THE RING

The shot put circle is 7 feet in diameter, usually constructed of concrete, with a wooden toe board at the front that is 4 feet long, 4 inches high, and 4½ inches wide. The ring is divided in half, and stepping out of the front half after a put constitutes a foul. Touching the top of the toe board, the circle, or the ground outside the circle is also a foul.

IDENTIFYING A POTENTIAL SHOT-PUTTER

If I could readily identify potential shot-putters, I would be the most successful shot put coach in the world. There are no pat criteria or formulas, but certain physical traits do stand out. Some of these were discussed in Chapters 8 and 9. The seven tests mentioned on page 169 can be a useful screening device. But if you're a coach, you should also look for these innate physical qualities in the prospective shot-putter:

Does he or she have explosive speed? The vertical jump, standing long jump, and 50-yard dash will tell you this.

What kind of basic strength does the individual possess? The dead lift, half squat, and bench press are great indicators, but keep in mind that good prospects should also have decent hand size and hand strength. Squeeze their hand as though you really mean it, and if they do not return the squeeze, challenge them: "Is that all the hand strength you have?" If the individual does not, or cannot, attack your hand with a vengeance after that, then I would say that he or she is definitely not cut out to be a shot-putter. Putters must be aggressive! But don't forget what was mentioned earlier: throwers come in all shapes and sizes. You owe it to the enthusiastic prospect, no matter what his body type, to give him a chance and to make that chance fun and challenging.

GETTING STARTED IN THE SHOT PUT

The purpose of the various movements in the ring is to create enough momentum to make that heavy shot weigh less. As long as the ball is moving in one direction, you won't have so much weight to put. Change direction and the weight increases. In the glide method, the shot should travel at a 40- to 45-degree angle from the moment you begin the put, rather than moving horizontally across the ring and then suddenly up at 45 degrees on release (which is what happens with the rotation method). Speed across the ring is important to give the shot momentum, but only as much speed as you can control.

Hold the shot deep in your hand, on the pads at the base of your fingers, with the thumb in front for balance and support. Keeping the weight too far out on the fingers could seriously injure them and your arm. Squeeze the shot lightly for added control. To help keep your elbow in the correct position (behind the shot), turn your hand out as you cradle the shot in the hollow between your neck and collarbone. The thumb is down, elbow up, and away from the body, and the palm is out, with pressure applied against the neck to hold the shot in. Pressure may also be applied by clamping the jawbone down on the top of the shot to help in stabilizing it during the glide across the ring. For a rotary throw some athletes like to hold the shot higher, between the ear and the base of the neck, but the hand and elbow positions do not necessarily change.

The following routines are exercises that will allow you to concentrate on one element of the technique at a time. During each practice session you will take several puts from a standing position, then several step-and-puts to add a little momentum, and finally several puts using the full motion across the ring.

Gripping the Shot

Hold the shot deep in the hand, on the pads at the base of your fingers. Keep your thumb in front for support, and squeeze the shot lightly for added control (right). Do not attempt to hold the shot on your fingertips, as this could injure hand and arm muscles.

Turn your hand out as you cradle the shot in the hollow between your neck and collarbone. This keeps your elbow behind the shot, where it belongs (below). Rotary throwers often like to hold the shot higher, between the ear and the base of the neck.

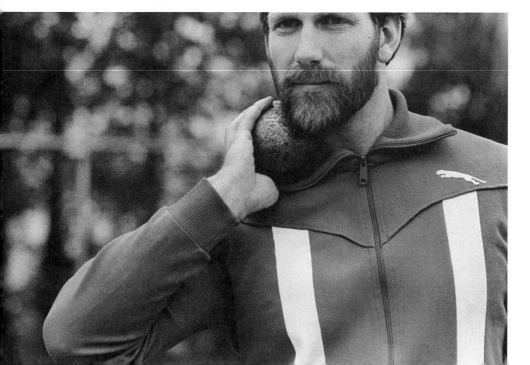

The Standing Put

Stand near the front of the ring, sideways to the direction of the put. Brace the ball and toes of your left foot lightly against the toe board, while your right foot is about in the center of the ring, perpendicular to the direction of the put.

Your hips, knees, and torso are aligned over your right leg, which is slightly bent at the knee in a half-squat position. Your shoulders, however, should be squared with the back of the ring, and you should be leaning toward the back of the ring in a slight crouch, but with your back straight. In this position, you should feel a certain "comfortable" tension in your torso.

Place the shot in position next to your chin. Your lead (left) arm, which maintains your balance, should be hanging down or reaching across to your right. As you begin the put, settle over your right leg. By pivoting on the ball of the foot, your right foot starts the turn, you push off your right leg, your torso lifts, and your left arm leads your body around. As your weight shifts and you begin to straighten over your left leg, your left arm pulls in sharply and your right arm simultaneously punches the shot out.

The sequence to remember at all times is turn–lift–punch. Your right leg should be lifting and turning before your torso starts to turn. The series of movements in the standing put represent what you want to approximate after a full ring crossing. The instant before the shot is punched, when your chest is stretched by the sharp pulling back of the left arm and your legs are driving in the push, is called the Bow.

Now take two to four puts from the standing position, emphasizing the lift: Do everything as described above, but leave your putting arm and hand on your shoulder. The shot will not go very far, but the distance is not important (when you're working on technique, don't worry about distance). You should be concentrating on getting the maximum lift from your right leg and thrust from your right hip. When it leaves your hand, the shot should be propelled only by the force of your body.

Next, take two to four puts while letting your hand and arm follow through on the release. Don't push or exert any force with your arm; merely follow the shot. What you're working on here is the turn—the pulling of your lead (left) arm and the thrust from straightening over your left leg.

Finally, take two to four puts emphasizing the punch. On the third or fourth put, practice exhaling explosively at the moment of delivery. As the ball leaves your hand, let your fingers snap out, with the thumb down and the elbow up.

The standing put.

Stand near the front of the ring, sideways to the direction of the put (A). Your right foot should be perpendicular to the direction of the put; the toes of your left foot should be lightly braced against the toe board. Holding the shot against your jaw and clavicle as shown here, align your hips, knees, and torso over your right leg, which is slightly bent. Square your shoulders with the back of the ring, and lean toward the back of the ring in a slight crouch, but with your back straight. Your left arm hangs down, as shown, to maintain balance. Now pivot on the ball of your right foot, push up on your right leg, lift your torso, and lead your body around with your left arm (B). As your weight shifts and you begin to straighten over your left leg, your left arm pulls in sharply and your right arm punches the shot upward and outward (C, D).

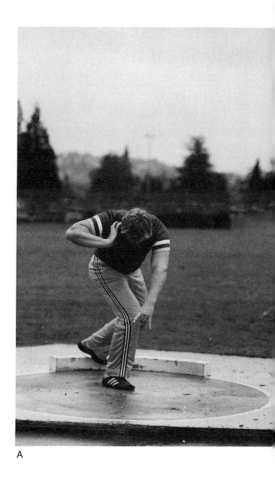

A

The Step-and-Put

Stand at the back of the ring, facing the direction of the put, with both knees slightly bent. Your lead arm is held out in front at 30 to 40 degrees; the shot is in position next to your neck. Step forward with your right foot, keeping your knee slightly bent, and turn your foot so that it's at about a 90-degree angle to the direction of the put. Settle over your right leg as your left leg comes forward (you should now be in a position similar to that of the standing put), and execute the put as described earlier. The main thing you're doing in the step-and-put is adding more momentum to the shot. Proceed to work on each of the elements described in the standing put, taking two to four puts on each.

The drills at the end of the chapter can also help you get started. Practice

B   C   D

until you feel comfortable with them, and with the standing put and the step-and-put. Only then should you move on to more advanced technique.

THE SHOT PUT TECHNIQUE

In my opinion there is little doubt that the future of the shot put lies in the rotation method rather than the glide. However, let me hasten to add that not every athlete possesses the skills and temperament necessary to be a rotational thrower, and there have been and will continue to be some excellent glide throwers who will be champions and world-record-holders. But I think the greatest *potential* is in the rotation method. If you're unsure of your choice of technique, don't limit yourself to the glide just because you may be small and lacking vast reserves of strength; rotational throwers come in many and varied body types. Yet there are some major differences between rotary and glide throwers that are noteworthy and that in some cases can be tested for, so one does not have to rely totally on trial and error. The rotary thrower is first of all a gambler—he or she cannot be intimidated by the board or by a foul throw. Second, good rotary throwers tend to possess a better vertical jump than the glide thrower, and therefore have more explosiveness behind their throws by virtue of innate leg strength. Third, good rotary throwers tend to sense the ring better with their feet as compared to the glide thrower.

THE GLIDE METHOD

As mentioned, I prefer the rotary method of moving across the ring. But I also realize that this technique requires tremendous leg and lower back strength, as well as a special sense of rhythm or "feel." Not all shot-putters may be up to the rotary method. Not to worry. The glide method reduces the likelihood of beginners' errors that cause imbalance and poor positioning in the center of the ring. If you feel more comfortable performing the glide, stick to it. Whatever you do, don't risk injury or inordinate frustration trying to do something that at best feels uncomfortable and at worst impossible.

Shot-putting great Al Fuerbach starts in a low position (as will be described), but he extends his left, or lead, leg. He then brings the left leg into the position described below and glides across the ring.

Parry O'Brien, father of the modern shot put and Olympic gold medal winner in 1952 and '56, started in an upright position, then bent forward and settled into the position described below. As you'll see if you experiment, there is much more rhythm in these styles than in the "static" position delineated here.

The Shot-Putter's Starting Position

To start the glide, stand at the rear of the ring, your back to the toe board, and position the shot against your neck. If you are a right-handed thrower, drop down on a flexed right knee, with your back rounded and almost parallel to the ground, and your left knee alongside the right. Your body mass must be located over the ball of your right foot, even though it may appear that your foot is flat on the ground. Indeed, most of your weight should be on your right foot, with the remainder on the toes of your left. Your shoulders should be hunched and your knees bent at approximately 120 degrees. Your left hand, dangling and relaxed, should hang palm out (to keep the left shoulder in) near, or touching, the toes of the right foot.

The Glide or Shift

Start your glide to the center of the circle by shifting your hips back so that the weight moves from the ball of the right foot to the heel. At the same time your left foot starts moving backward. Now your right and left legs should begin the drive simultaneously: Extend your right leg from the heel upward, and extend your left leg straight back, toward the toe board. Your shoulders and hips must stay square with the back of the circle until the right foot lifts from the throwing surface. If you initiate the glide by straightening your right leg completely from the toes, your right foot will not drag to the center of the circle. If you extend your left leg completely in order to bring your left foot up against the toe board, your hip will not slide laterally as you go into the power position. At the end of the glide, your hips and trunk will rise naturally to allow the right foot to slide to the center of the circle. Some modern glide throwers, incidentally, tend to be more upright in the center than their predecessors— something we discuss next.

The Power Position

Once the right foot leaves the ground, the hips, right foot, and left foot rotate so that the toes of the left foot are against the toe board and the right foot is approximately in the center of the circle, at a 90-degree angle to the left foot. To use a baseball analogy, if the right foot was in the back of the batter's box, the left would be slightly in the bucket. The shoulders are still square with the back of the circle. The supporting foot strikes the center of the circle, hard, and continues to rotate forward along with the knee, which is bent at approximately a 120-degree angle. The left leg and foot are still extended and only slightly bent and touching the toe board. You should *drive* into the toe board with your left foot—do not hop!! You are now in what is known as the Power Position.

The Put

As the right foot and hip begin to rotate forward, your center of mass is moved forward onto the left leg. This means the left leg bends at the knee at an angle of approximately 120 degrees. In the power position the free arm and shoulder have opened slightly, which is natural and should be allowed to happen, and the right shoulder and arm stay back. At this moment, if the shot were dropped

194 straight down, it would land just outside the right foot (but don't drop the shot this way to check your technique, lest you be out of position and injure your foot as a result).

As your rotational force moves forward, your free arm should straighten and move to a point parallel with the shoulders. Your center of mass is still down.

Now it's time to . . . *get violent!* Rotate your trunk forward to a point where it is square with the toe board. Your free arm can aid this motion by shortening its own radius—bending at the elbow. Straighten both legs upward, with the left blocking any continued forward movement. Your right hip should be well forward by now, and your hips are square with the board (this is the Bow position, described earlier). Blocking with the left leg naturally imparts greater speed to the shot by allowing the right shoulder to follow through on the throw. The throwing angle is 39 to 40 degrees. Keep your chin and chest up, and from the corner of your right eye, watch the shot leave your hand.

The shot will actually seem to pull away from your neck to your throwing shoulder. The shot should leave your hand with the thumb down, elbow up, and with a very forceful outward snap of the wrist and fingers.

Putting the Shot: The Glide Method

The crouch.

The reach with the left foot.

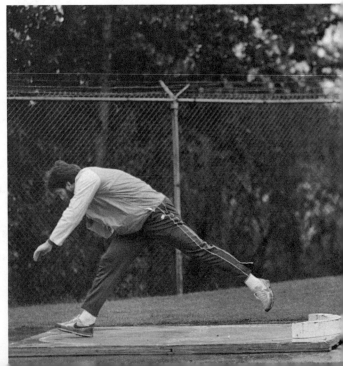

The Reverse, or Follow-Through

The finish, or reverse, is a natural movement—the result of following through. Once the shot has left your hand, your throwing arm continues across your body, and your foot positions change: your right foot moves to the front and into the toe board, and the left foot moves to the rear. To keep from fouling (stepping over the toe board), let your right foot strike the board, toes first, and then immediately lower your center of mass by bending your knee.

I have often compared a shot-putter to a boxer—the requirements for both are quick feet and hands. In the case of shot-putting, you need a quick right foot to the center of the ring and an explosive right hand on the finish.

Be relaxed at the start, and concentrate on making your feet quick. In the center of the ring, stay down and rotate, then *explode* with both legs on the finish. Start the throw with a continuous rotation of the right foot, knee, hip, and free arm, and when you actually make the put, remember: chin and chest *up!*

The block with the left leg.   The put.

The follow-through onto the right leg.

THE ROTARY, OR ROTATION, METHOD

The rotational thrower innately has quick feet, possesses a good sense of balance, and is aggressive. The advantages of the rotation throw for this type of athlete include (1) a longer acceleration path, (2) faster acceleration in the delivery phase, and (3) a higher angle of release (the direct result of better lift with both legs).

The dangers of the method include (1) a greater chance of fouling than with the glide and (2) a greater chance of body imbalance during the movement across the center of the ring. Successful rotary throws depend, first and foremost, on a proper start. Let's look at this phase closely.

The Start

Facing the back of the ring, start in a comfortable crouch with your weight evenly balanced on both feet, your shoulders level and rotated to the right so that they and your head are turned somewhat toward the front (toe board), and your left leg is back and balancing its share of the weight on the ball of the foot. Now move your head and left shoulder sideways to a point over the left foot, so that your weight shifts onto that foot and—most important—your right foot rises at the same time. Swing your right leg wide so that if you were to stop, your body mass would be well outside the left leg and in a balanced position, not falling or leaning into the center from the left side. This means that your head and left shoulder must stop moving to allow your right foot and leg to lead into the center of the ring.

The Sprint into the Throw

At this point you become a sort of sprinter. From a wide position over your left (supporting) leg, your right leg and foot flex and plant in the center of the ring. *Drive* your right foot into the center; you want to get off the left leg quickly, just as the right foot descends, hard, into the center. Your trunk is relatively vertical and remains vertical to a point where, if the shot were dropped now, it would land closer to the right foot than during the similar movement in the glide. Your free arm should act as a balancing or stabilizing agent for the left foot; ideally the free arm should *not* lead the body into the next phase.

The Power Position

The center position for the rotary method is somewhat like that for the glide, except that the knees are spread well apart once rotation starts, the head and right shoulder are angled back, and you rotate on the balls of both feet.

After this point, everything is the same as with the glide. You step forward with your left foot, press it against the toe board, block with your left leg, square your hips with the board, throw your chest and chin upward, and explode up and out with your throw. This is an emotional moment—scream your head off! Don't keep that energy bottled up.

PLANNING A TRAINING PROGRAM

Here is a recommended practice progression to follow when training for the shot put.

Stretches

Before a throwing workout, and especially after a weight training session, you should do the following basic stretching exercises:

The Opposite-Hand Toe-Touch. Stand with your feet spread, and raise your arms to shoulder level at your sides. Bend at the waist and touch your left foot with your right hand, then your right foot with your left hand. Do this exercise two ways: (1) returning to the upright position, arms out, between touches; and (2) remaining bent at the waist and moving only the arms at the shoulder. As one hand sweeps across and down, the other should stretch up and back. Do each version 10 times.

The Hurdler's Stretch. Resting the knee and the inside of the lower leg on a track hurdle or similar horizontal support at your side, maintain a straight free leg, toes straight ahead, and reach down along it with your outside hand until you can grasp your ankle, or until you can feel the stretch along your side and the insides of your legs. Do not bounce; keep the stretch passive. Hold for 8 seconds and repeat, switching legs.

Putting the Shot: The Rotary, or Rotation, Method

The start.
The weight shift onto the left foot.

The plant of the right foot and reach with the left leg.
The block with the left leg.

The swing with the right leg.

The put.

The follow-through.

 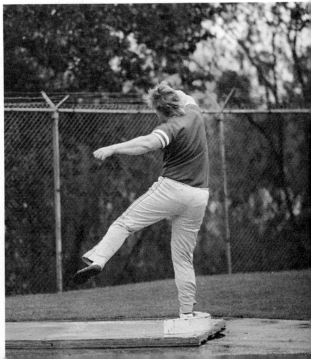

200

The Groin Stretch (static). Sit on the ground and draw your feet together at the soles. Now round your back and grasp your ankles, and using your elbows, apply outward pressure to your knees and lower legs. Keep your head down. You'll feel the stretch along the muscles and tendons of the groin and inner leg. Again, no bouncing; keep the stretch passive. Hold the stretch for 8 seconds, and repeat several times.

The Inverted Bicycle Stretch (static). Lie on your back, and keeping your arms flat on the ground, raise your legs over your head. Keep your legs straight. Then slowly reach back over your head with your feet, and try to touch the ground with your toes. Repeat 6 times—and again, no bouncing. This position stretches the upper and lower back, the neck, and the hamstrings.

The Hamstring Stretch (static). From a standing position, spread your feet slightly, toes straight ahead or slightly out, and with both hands slowly reach down and grasp one ankle. Feel the stretch along the hamstrings and calf muscles in the back of your leg. Hold for 8 seconds. Repeat for a total of 6 times for each leg.

The Hamstring Stretch II (static). Lie on your back with your legs out straight. Bend one leg at the knee, and draw it toward your chest with your hands. Hold the position for 8 seconds, keeping your head on the ground. Then do the same with the other leg, then both legs together. Besides the hamstrings, this exercise stretches the muscles of the lower back.

The Pretzel. Sit on the ground with one leg extended in front, and lift the opposite foot over the extended knee and place it on the ground. Now gently turn your upper body in the direction of the bent leg, and use your hands to pull the bent knee toward your chest. Hold the stretch for 8 seconds, then work the other side of your body. Repeat 6 times. This exercise stretches the sides of the hips, the lumbar area (lower back), the abdomen, and the lower rib cage.

The Toe Touch. From a standing position with knees locked, toes straight ahead, reach down and slowly touch your toes. Straighten. Repeat for a total of 6 times. Your head should hang loose and you should feel as if you are "rolling" down and up along the spine. This exercise stretches the calf and hamstring muscles, which are susceptible to pulls and tears.

The pretzel.

Drills

The purpose of these drills is to train you to "explode" from the squat position during the shot put. Your muscle reactions and actions must be quick and explosive—not slow and methodical—and you should do these drills at every throwing practice.

Sometimes using a heavier shot is beneficial in these drills, but only during the off-season. At Washington we have experimented with a lighter shot for drills and for throwing during the season and have had very good results, especially when a thrower is trying to overcome some persistent form faults.

The Over-the-Head Toss. Firmly cradling the shot in both hands close to your lower abdomen, assume a full squat. Using the legs and back first, explode upward and backward, tossing the shot behind you, over your head, and coming off the ground at the end of the movement. Repeat 6 times.

The Throw Over Each Side. Again firmly cradling the shot close to your hips, rise upward from a squat but less explosively than in the over-the-head toss, and toss the shot over one shoulder. Repeat on the other side. Work on smooth, controlled upper body rotation. Repeat 6 to 8 times each side.

The Underhand Toss. Everything in this exercise is the same as with the over-the-head toss, only here the shot is thrown up and forward, from the underhand position, not up and over the head.

The Squat Push. Just like the over-the-head toss, except here the shot is "pushed" forward with both hands, as in a basketball pass. Raise the chest to a 45-degree angle and make the push at the same angle.

The Flip. This drill helps develop wrist and hand strength. With your hips and feet facing the toe board, hold the shot deep in your hand, in the standard neck position, cock your wrist to keep your elbow behind the shot, and without exerting too much force, flip the shot forward. Do 6 to 8 repetitions.

Release and Rotation. Now do the flip with somewhat more force, concentrating on good follow-through and rotation both with the free (left) hand and the right shoulder. The right shoulder should follow through in the throw by actually moving beyond the plane of the toe board. This is an excellent drill for learning proper rotation, as well as use of the left arm and right shoulder. Do 6 to 8 repetitions.

Stands. Assume the power position. Now, using both legs to start the throw, lift your body up and rotate into the release. Your right foot and front knee should pivot, and your left leg is flexed at a 120-degree angle as you go into the throw. Practice first with no reverse, then allow a complete finish. Do 6 to 8 repetitions.

Glide Drills. These drills are designed to help develop quick feet. In the first exercise, start with both feet together at the back of the ring, and using standard glide throwers' movements, drive backward off both feet, landing in a balanced position in the center of the ring. Repeat 15 to 20 times.

In the second exercise, start by repeating the first, but land in the power position (see page 193). Your hips and feet therefore must rotate on the drive back, your shoulders remain square with the back of the circle, and your left foot and hip open up.

The Glide. The main point of this drill is to work on your start and glide into the center of the ring. Instead of a shot, hold a wadded-up towel or a softball, but concentrate on your form and speed, not on whatever you are holding. Now go through the choreography of the start and glide, as outlined on pages 192–195.

The Put. Practice the actual put with a shot while concentrating on the major elements of all the previous drills. Strive to perform the choreography of the put perfectly. However, don't concentrate on more than one or two elements of technique per practice session; trying to deal with more only leads to confusion, frustration, and possible injury. Repeat the put as many times as you can *but without sacrificing proper technique.*

COACHING TIPS
FOR THE SHOT PUT

- Look for *causes* of technique problems in your shot-putter—that is, for cause-and-effect relationships in his shot-putting.
- Check for balance throughout the putter's start, middle, and finish.
- Remind the putter that the total throwing movement originates from the hips and legs.
- Remember, too, that the shot put is a *linear* event. Rotation takes place along a line in both techniques.
- Feet! Feet! Feet! The shot-putter's feet should stay close to the surface of the ring—don't hop across! His feet should be quick. Like a boxer's, his feet must be planted to deliver a knockout blow. His right foot and knee should pivot in the center of the circle; they shouldn't drag.
- When in the power-position, the putter shouldn't bend at the hips. His body should extend in a straight line from the extended left leg, through the hips, to the top of the head.
- Study the relationship of the shot-putter's left arm and right hip. Do they move together?
- Check the putter's chin-chest relationship—the chin stays in the middle of the chest such that the putter can watch the shot leave his hand.
- Does the shot-putter block with his left arm and leg? At the moment of the throw, his entire left side should be immobilized.
- At the start and midpoint of his motion (in the center of the ring), are the shot-putter's hips balanced over the right heel?
- Remember, as the putter's left leg extends on the glide, his weight moves from over the toes to the ball of the right foot.
- Note the trunk position of the thrower during the glide, center, and finish phases of the throw. Refer to pages 192–195 for proper positioning.
- When the thrower releases the shot put, look for (1) proper body angle (blocking position), (2) the lifting action of both legs, and (3) the action of the left arm and right shoulder (does the left arm move freely into the throw, and does the right shoulder extend into and through the shot on the finish?).
- Does the thrower assume the power position, or does he slide through it? Watch for hip slide and try to correct it immediately.

11

The Discus Throw

In track and field, every event has its own rhythm. Perhaps none is more obvious than that of the discus. Years ago, when I was competing, my coach had me practice the discus to the music of different records—slow, fast, syncopated, three-quarter time, swing. You name it, I threw to it. The purpose? To get me to understand the rhythmic feel of the discus motion. "Shannon," he used to yell at me, "forget what your arm is doing. Forget about generating power. Just experience the rhythm of the event. Be a dancer! Not a bull in a china shop!" His thoughts about rhythm and the discus took a little getting used to, because frankly my feelings about dancing were not very enlightened then.

Still, though, my coach was right: You do have to feel the rhythm of the discus. It's a rhythm that's been part of the event since the time of the ancient Greeks—and very few ideas about the discus, mine included, are new and original. Mine are borrowed from time-tested collective and personal experience, including what I gained as a beginner, throwing in a cow pasture with my dad. My family and I lived in a remote area of the Sierra Nevada mountains, and my father had thrown the hammer and the discus in college. His early lessons in the discus gave me a feel for the event, which I try to pass on to my students today. In all, my dad's gentle urgings got me started in both football and track, and the hundreds of hours spent throwing (or as often as not, trying to find the thrown discus buried in the mud of an irrigation pond) really paid off for me in college. Not only did I enter college a good thrower, but my skills won me an athletic scholarship.

My other ideas about the discus have been gained from clinics, from talking with coaches, and, mostly, from listening to and watching elite athletes.

205

The discus is perhaps the most rhythmic of the
throwing events.

Every season brings new ideas, and I try to incorporate these into my throwers' individual training programs. And yet, when it comes to teaching the discus, my heart and mind go back to that scrubby cow pasture where my father taught me the basics, and to my college's throwing circle, where my coach gave me a sense of my favorite event's rhythm and grace. It's rhythm and certain basics more than any fancy innovation that a discus thrower must know. For us coaches, the trick lies in making those basics work for each athlete.

THE BIOMECHANICS OF THE DISCUS THROW

The underlying biomechanical requirements for throwing the discus well are muscular strength and speed. The quicker you can unleash the appropriate muscular strength, the faster and farther you'll throw the discus. Listen to K. Metsuer, throwing coach for the U.S.S.R., on the subject: "Good throwing distances are achieved when the muscle groups involved perform with maximal strength in a minimum time. At the same time, because of muscle viscosity, it is impossible to use all available strength at once. Consequently, the deciding factor is not enormous strength but the athlete's ability to mobilize the available strength step by step in the shortest time. In other words, the shorter the time taken to mobilize the strength, the faster the movement speed."

One of the most common mistakes made by beginning discus throwers trying to harness their muscles' speed is that of "bringing down the rain"— firing out of control from the hip at such an angle that the discus heads for the sky. While this is fine for seeding clouds, it doesn't score any points in an event that measures distance horizontally. So in going for muscle speed, you must learn to sling the discus out, not up.

Another word of caution while we're on the subject of flying objects: Because beginners have a tendency to let go with some wild efforts (even elite athletes are not immune to this problem), it's best to keep the throwing area clear and to make sure that everyone in the area is alert when someone is practicing the event. A flying discus to the head is no laughing matter.

The throwing motion in the discus is very fluid and flowing. Rhythmically, it is not as explosive as the shot put, in part because the thrower is working in a larger ring (8 feet 2½ inches). As Metsuer points out, it is not enormous strength that propels the discus great distances, but instead the thrower's ability to accelerate the speed of the discus throughout the entire motion in the ring, and to finish explosively. Therefore, a discus thrower's muscles must be very elastic, especially in the upper body, and the muscles of the legs, back, and torso must be especially strong and quick. Remember, if you *are* strong, quickness will naturally follow.

Like the javelin, which we'll discuss in the next chapter, the discus has unique aerodynamic qualities that you must understand in order to improve your performance in the event. Stated simply, the more weight there is on the circumference of the discus (as provided by its metal rim), the faster it will rotate, because it will leave the hand with more force.

THE IMPLEMENT

The discus is a plate-shaped wooden or synthetic body framed by a metal rim (for safety, many high schools use a discus made of rubber), with the following dimensions:

> Women: 2 pounds 3½ ounces, 7⅛ to 7¼ inches in diameter
>
> High school men: 3 pounds 9 ounces, 8½ inches in diameter
>
> Collegiate men: 4 pounds 5½ ounces, 8⅝ to 8¾ inches in diameter

Both sides of a discus are the same, with a slight taper from the center to the rim, but some discuses have more weight concentrated on the rim than others. The best way to find a discus that's right for you is to experiment, throwing several models in your category until you find the one you're most comfortable with.

As with the shot put, the transition for men from throwing the 3¾-pound discus in high school to throwing the 4½-pound version in college can be tough. A 190-foot thrower in high school, for instance, can expect to throw about 170 feet in college. Once again, you must be patient, concentrate on proper technique, and learn to throw with your body, not just your arm.

THE RING

The discus is thrown from within a circle (8 feet 2½ inches) in diameter, made of band iron or steel sunk into concrete. As in the shot put, it is considered a foul to step out of the front half of the ring after a throw. A good practice surface may be made from ¾-inch plywood painted with latex mixed with fine sand.

THE GRIP

There are three grips commonly used by discus throwers, and each is dependent on the thrower's hand size and strength. The first is the *standard* grip, in which all fingers are evenly spread; the second is the *talon,* or *claw,* grip, in which the fingers are closer together; and the third is a *variation* of the standard in which the index and middle finger are together. The aim of each grip is to provide a hold on the discus that will create a clockwise rotation for a right-hander (a counterclockwise one for a left-hander) and ensure a stable flight. In the standard position, the discus is placed in the palm of the hand, with the fingers and thumb comfortably spread. The rim of the discus rests against the pads above the first joints of the four fingers. South African John Van Reenan, of Washington State University, has the biggest and strongest hands of any discus thrower I've ever seen. Ludvik Danek of Czechoslovakia has the second biggest. Their hands literally engulf the discus, and they generally use the standard grip when they throw. Smaller-handed throwers tend to use the claw or talon to facilitate more rotation on the release, while those with average-size hands might move the first and second fingers closer together for the same purpose (the variation grip). Which grip is right for you? The only way you'll find out is to experiment, both by yourself and with the help of your coach.

Whatever grip you choose, hold the discus at the ends of your fingers. Power comes from the first and second fingers, although the discus should fly off the index finger for a more stable flight. You may use your opposite hand to keep the discus in place at the top of your preliminary swing (more later). Practice, rolling the discus off your index finger and throwing it in the air until you get the feel of it. As you'll quickly see, basic strength in the hand, wrist, and forearm is a necessity when throwing the discus. Power lifting (the dead lift, clean, and snatch—see pages 174–178) can enhance hand strength, but I like throwers who have worked hard as youngsters at chopping wood, using a shovel, and other forms of manual labor. Obviously not all youngsters can have these experiences, so to every thrower I say hit the weights.

The Grip

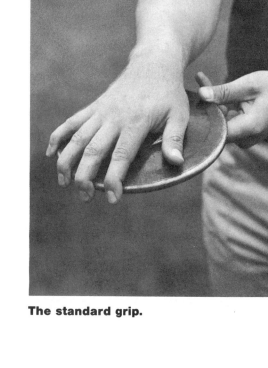

The standard grip.

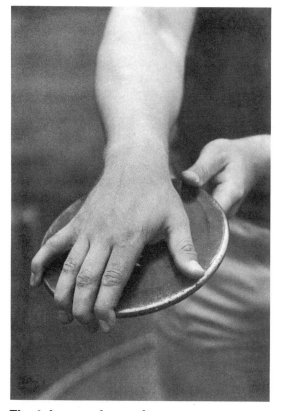

The talon, or claw, grip.

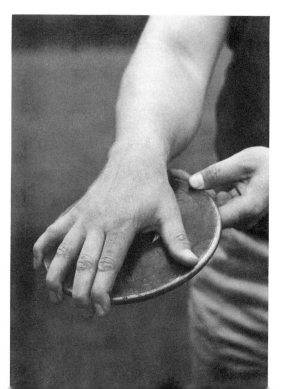

The power grip.

**GETTING STARTED
IN THE DISCUS**

The Standing Throw

Stand at the front of the ring, sideways to the direction of the throw and facing to the right if you are right-handed, your feet are about shoulder width apart; your right foot is in the center of the ring and turned at a right angle to the direction of the throw. Your left foot is pointing slightly left of center so your hips will have room to turn into the throw. Practice rocking back and forth, swinging the discus as far to the right as is comfortable. Keep your right arm as extended as possible. This is a wind-up for the throw. For balance and control, you shouldn't have to take more than one or two swings.

In order to get your whole body behind each effort, the throw must begin from the ground up. Your right foot starts the turn, followed by your right leg and hip as your left arm swings out and then pulls in at the elbow. As your weight shifts to your left leg, you should get power and lift from that leg. All of this occurs *before* your right arm brings the discus around. This is the bow or power position (more later). Now, with your chest up, bring your arm around for an easy release. Practice the standing throw 18 to 20 times, so that swinging the discus and moving into the power position feels comfortable.

The Step-and-Throw

After practicing the standing throw so that it begins to feel natural, you're ready to try the step-and-throw. This adds momentum. From the back of the ring, face in the direction of the throw. With your right foot, step forward to the center of the circle as you swing the discus up, then step to the left with your left foot and get into position over your right leg as the discus comes all the way back. Concentrate on keeping your shoulders level: too much dip will mean that the discus is released at too steep an angle. You want it to go at an angle of 34 to 40 degrees. Using the thrust of your right leg and hip, and the sharp pull of the bent left arm, bring the discus around and release. Practice the step-and-throw until all the motions feel integrated and comfortable. Once you've learned the standing throw and the step-and-throw, you're ready to move on to more advanced techniques.

The Starting Position

The most important quality you should develop as a discus thrower, and one possessed by the modern discus greats—Wolfgang Schmidt of East Germany, Ludvik Danek of Czechoslovakia, Fortune Gordein, and Jay Sylvester, Mac Wilkens, and John Powell of the United States—is balance. Since you should sprint, not spin, across the ring to make your throw, balance plays a crucial role in successfully converting your linear motion into a throw.

Stand at the back of the ring, facing away from the direction of the throw.

Foot position for the start of the discus.
Facing away from the direction of the throw, your left foot is near the edge of the ring, your right foot slightly back.

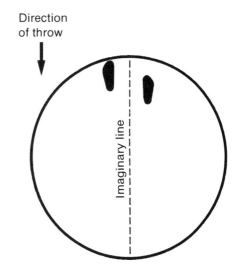

Your feet are about shoulder width apart, your left foot on or near an imaginary line running from the back to the front of the ring, your right foot slightly back, your weight evenly balanced on both feet. Begin the rocking motion as you start your wind-up. When your weight is on your right foot, the discus should be around back to the right as far as possible. The shoulders are level with the head and chest, and the left arm is held shoulder high, relaxed, and somewhat across the body, which is erect, not bent at the waist. The throw begins with the left leg: it bends and starts to turn left so that the weight is on the ball of the left foot and your center of mass is directly underneath you.

The next step is to move the left shoulder sideways, counterclockwise. At the same time, the right foot is lifted from the circle. Your weight is now centered on the inside of the rotating left foot and knee. Your right leg should sweep as wide as it can (the degree of leg sweep varies for each thrower) and the discus remains well back and up—at almost a 90-degree angle to the ground for some throwers.

The Sprint Across the Ring

You begin the sprint by pushing off the left foot and landing on the ball of your right foot. To enable the right foot and leg to swing wide and then drive, or sprint, into the center, you should pause briefly—"block," if you will—before you lift your right foot from the circle. To further facilitate the sprint onto the right foot, pretend that you are jumping off the left foot and onto the right. It may not appear to an observer that you are actually jumping, but by trying to do so, you accomplish an important purpose: you sprint off the left foot rather than spin off it.

Again, the right leg should swing wide. As it passes to the left of the imaginary line dividing the ring, it drives down and across the left leg into the center of the circle. In other words it moves from a position wide of the body to one close to, or nearly underneath it. This move elevates the discus so that the right shoulder is higher than the left and, overall, a crucial position is attained, one that I look for in all high school throwers I might recruit—that is, the shoulders and the arms are all parallel to the direction of the throw. Your position at this point, in the middle of the turn, is the reciprocal of what your position will be at the release. Crossing the right leg close to the left leg also helps enable you to get the left leg across the ring and to the front of the circle *quickly.* The wider you cross with the right leg, the slower the left advances across the ring.

Once your right foot strikes the center of the circle, the motion is similar to that for the shot put. Your momentum should carry you all the way around on the rotating right foot and knee. As you come around to the front of the ring, plant your left foot (pointing slightly left of center). This stops, or blocks, your turn and creates the whip action necessary for the actual throw.

The Power Position

As your right foot and knee rotate around, your entire right leg and hip should be pushing into the power position, with your right foot pointing forward. Your body's center of mass is still down; the discus remains at a 90-degree angle; both feet are actually rotating. Just as in the shot put, this is when you have to get violent. Your trunk rotates forward to a position where it is stretched square with the front of the circle. Your free arm aids this motion by shortening its radius (bending at the elbow). Both legs straighten, with the left leg now blocking any further forward movement. Indeed, the entire left side should feel immobilized. Your right hip is well forward of the right shoulder and hand. The blocking action helps impart greater speed to the discus by allowing the right shoulder and hand to follow through on the throw. Now your right arm whips around and you release the discus. The throwing angle is 34 to 40 degrees, with the height of release dependent on your size and leg strength. Keep your chin and chest up, and from the corner of your eye, briefly watch the discus leave your hand.

It's important to note that the throwing arm and hand are at a 90-degree angle with the shoulder, and the hand is flat. If you throw right-handed, the spinning motion of the discus is counterclockwise and, if you've done everything properly, fast. Your thumb acts as a guide, preventing the discus from fluttering and promoting a smooth flight. The palm of your hand remains flat on the discus, with the wrist straight.

The Finish

The finish, or reverse, is a natural motion. Your throwing arm follows through, across and down the body, your feet change positions, and as the right foot hits the ring surface, it immediately pivots counterclockwise. Once you release the discus, you should strive to lower your center of mass immediately, gain control of your body's motion, and only then watch the flight of the discus. I can't begin to count the number of throwers who have nullified a good throw by fouling because they forgot to get under control.

Throwing the Discus

A   B   C

To throw the discus, start by standing toward the back of the ring, your feet about shoulder width apart and positioned as shown in the illustration on page 211. Begin the rocking motion as you start your windup (A). When your weight is on your right foot, the discus should be around back as far as possible. The shoulders are level with the head and chest, and the left arm is about shoulder high, relaxed, and somewhat across the body (B, C).

D   E   F

Begin the throw by bending the left leg and starting to turn it to the left so that the weight is on the ball of the left foot and your center of mass is balanced on both feet and directly underneath you (D). Your left shoulder now moves sideways counterclockwise (E), and your right foot starts to lift from the circle (F).

(continued)

G   H   I

Your weight is now centered on the inside of the rotating left foot and knee. Sweep your right leg as wide as you can and keep the discus well back, almost at a 90-degree angle to the ground (G). You begin the sprint phase of the throw by pushing off the left foot and landing forward on your right foot (H, I), to the left of the imaginary centerline. Your momentum now carries you all the way around on your rotating right foot and knee (J). As you come around to the front of the ring, plant your left foot, pointing it slightly left of center (K). This stops, or blocks, your turn and creates the whip action necessary for the actual throw. You are now in the Power Position, your throwing arm back, but your trunk rotated forward to a position where it is stretched square with the front of the circle. Your free arm aids this position by shortening its radius (bending at the elbow). Now, both legs straighten, and with the left leg blocking any further forward movement, your right arm whips around and you release the discus (L). The throwing angle is 34 to 40 degrees, and your chin and chest are up. From the corner of your eye, briefly watch the discus leave your hand. Your throwing arm follows through, across and down the body, your feet change positions, and as the right foot hits the ring surface, it immediately rotates counterclockwise, and you find yourself with your back to the throw. Time to lower your body's center of mass by flexing your knees to control your body's motion (M).

J

K

L

M

POINTS TO REMEMBER

• The rhythm of the discus is one of constantly increasing speed. You want to come gradually out of the back of the ring, but you want to be fast (only as fast as you can control) from the center of the ring to delivery.

• The discus will go in the direction your left foot is pointed.

• You want the outer edge of the discus to be banked slightly to the right (tilted slightly toward the ground) so the flight will be horizontal (the spin on release will make it tend to turn over).

• Beware of firing from the hip—the discus should be released at an angle of 34 to 40 degrees.

• Success in the discus depends entirely upon your learning to sprint off the left foot, not spin off it, and to drive the right leg down and into the center of the circle. The only real rotation takes place while you move into the power position.

DRILLS

Some discus throwers use two implements to save time in the practice session. You might also put out pegs or shoes as targets to help you work on accuracy. The discus must be thrown within a 60-degree sector for high school competitors and a 40-degree sector for collegiate and open throwers, so you don't want wild throws in competition.

You and your coach should be able to develop a training program for the discus by consulting the training recommendations for the shot put on pages 197–203. In addition, here are some event-specific drills that can help you attain better form and distance in the discus. Each should be practiced 8 to 10 times.

The Left-Foot Drill

Holding the discus properly in your throwing hand, assume the starting position, go through the rocking motion, and concentrate on your push, or "snap," off the left foot. Your thighs should be close together as your center of mass passes onto the ball of the left foot, and the foot itself should make vigorous contact with the circle. Repeat the drill 8 to 10 times.

The Sprint Drill

The primary purpose of this drill is to learn the start of the movement into the power position. Again holding the discus properly, start at the back of the circle with your weight evenly balanced over both feet. Now move your left shoulder, counterclockwise, so that your weight is now dominant on the ball of your pivoting left foot. It is crucial that your left knee pivots ahead of your left shoulder. Pick your right foot off the circle, and begin the sprint by driving the right knee and foot (thighs close) into the center of the ring. Remember, think of yourself as hopping off the left foot, not spinning on it. Repeat 8 to 10 times.

The Half-Turn Drill

Sometimes called the South African Drill, this is designed (1) to develop the concept of jumping off the left foot, (2) to establish a wide base in the center of the ring, and (3) to develop a sense of the rotation required to go into the power position. Start with the left foot just inside the back of the circle, your body facing in the direction of the throw. With your throwing arm well back, step into the center of the ring with your right foot and at the same time sprint off your left foot. You are now in the power position and can proceed with your throw. Before your first step, you can take your usual number of preliminary rocking movements. Try to keep your hips down as you throw. They will come up naturally after your right foot rotates. Reach with your left foot for the front of the circle in order to secure a wide throwing base. Keep the throws easy. Repeat 8 to 10 times.

The Towel Drill

Using a towel as the instrument, go through your entire throw, concentrating on the accelerating rhythm of the throw, nothing else. If you'd like, do what my coach had me do: perform the drill to a variety of different musical styles.

ADDITIONAL STARTING POSITIONS

A Beginner's Start

This position helps the beginner achieve balance when he starts and in the power position:

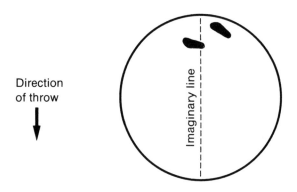

An Intermediate's Starting Position

As you become more confident in your throws, keep advancing your left foot toward the edge of the circle, like this:

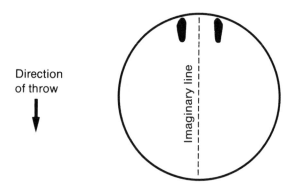

Three Advanced Starting Positions

The position described on page 211 is the second position here. There are three advanced starting positions. The farther back from the edge of the circle the right foot moves, the more proficient you must become in sprinting into the power position.

Direction of throw

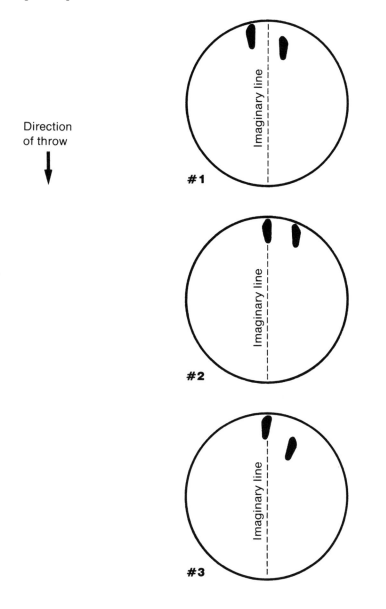

COACHING TIPS
FOR THE DISCUS THROW

• Look for causes of problems. An unbalanced power position, for example, with the thrower lurching sideways, is often the result of an unbalanced starting position.

• Check the thrower's balance in the back of the ring. After the thrower takes his preliminary swings, his weight should be balanced over his left foot in order to be able to jump and sprint into the power position.

• The total throwing motion originates from the legs and hips. Don't let the thrower get away with throwing with his upper body. Remember, too, that the discus, like the shot put, is a linear event, with rotation developed in the center of the circle. Do not let the thrower's hips slide into the power position. Watch to make sure the left leg blocks, straightening as the thrower rotates onto it.

• The thrower's upper body should remain vertical, not bent at the waist. The thrower should think of himself as "dragging" the discus into the center of the ring.

• The tempo of the throw should be: *One* (motion around the left foot at the start), *Two* (right foot strikes in center of ring), *Three* (left foot strikes at front of ring), with parts two and three quickly accelerating.

• The thrower's weight should be on the balls of his feet.

• His thighs should be close together on the sprint down and into the center of the circle.

• Watch the thrower's chin and chest at the moment of the throw. They should move upward together, not separately.

• Note the position of the thrower's left arm and right foot and hip at the start of the throwing motion. The left arm should be bent at the elbow; the right foot and hip should be square to the ring.

• The thrower's hips should remain level, both at the start (stay down!) and during the early phase of the rotation onto the left foot going into the power position.

• Study the thrower's power position. His weight should be held over the balls of both feet, with the weight concentrated mostly on the right foot. The shoulders should be square with the back of the circle, and the discus should be well back and up, with the throwing arm close to the right side of the trunk.

• Watch the thrower's entire left side at the finish. It should be immobile.

12

The Javelin Throw

To say the javelin is the most complex of all throwing events might seem insulting to all those who have worked so hard on the shot, discus, and hammer. Yet I don't think it's far from the truth, because to be a successful javelin thrower requires an intricate mix of speed, agility, coordination, and explosiveness. As in the shot put and the discus throw, the basic mechanics of linear and rotary motion, plus blocking action at the finish, all apply in the javelin, but much greater body speed is needed than for the other events. Reaction, timing, body balance (center of mass), are all crucial. As we shall see, you throw the javelin not just with the arm, but with the action of the entire body, concluding with a drawing together of all its forces into a whiplike fling with the throwing arm. In his excellent book *The Dynamics of the Javelin Throw,* Dr. Robert F. Sing describes the motion of the arm as "a crack of the whip"–type motion.

I once heard a fellow coach describe the javelin thrower as a "lean, mean machine" who would love to throw a rock a hundred yards a hundred times a day, or as a nice amiable person who, with a javelin in her hands, becomes "a maniac willing to start World War III" if she could use the javelin as a missile. Perhaps the latter analogy is farfetched, but the fact remains that the javelin thrower is a unique personality who, throughout the history of the event, has come in all shapes and sizes.

THE IMPLEMENT

The International Amateur Athletic Federation (IAAF), which is the governing body for track and field in the world, states in its rules: "The javelin consists of three parts: a metal head, a shaft, and a cord grip. The shaft may be

225

Throwing the javelin requires the action of the entire body, not just the arm.

constructed of metal and it shall have fixed to it a metal head terminating in a sharp point. The cord shall be located [in the area of the javelin's] center of gravity, without thongs, notches, or indentations of any kind. The javelin shall have no mobile parts or other apparatus that, during the throw, could change its center of gravity or throwing characteristics."

The length and weight of the javelin for men and women are as follows:

Length/Weight of Javelin	Men	Women
Maximum overall length:	8 feet 10.25 inches	7 feet 5.459 inches
Minimum overall length:	8 feet 6.375 inches	7 feet 2.178 inches
Maximum weight:	1 pound 12.25 ounces (800 grams)	1 pound 5.16 ounces (600 grams)

In 1986 changes in the taper of the shaft and position of the grip were instituted by the IAAF out of concern that the men's javelin was being thrown too far and therefore was not safe. The grip on the new javelin has been moved 2 inches forward, and its tail does not taper to a point as much or as soon as the old javelin. In other words, the new javelin is fatter over a longer distance compared to the old one. The result: when it loses momentum, the new javelin tends to "tip over" sooner and fall to the ground earlier. The appearance of this new javelin has caused a severe drop in the distances the javelin is thrown. Where once the world record in the event was some 340 feet, it is currently just over 280 feet—a 60-foot reduction in distance!

Any javelin in careless hands is a dangerous weapon. To prevent accidents, always take the following precautions: (1) Make sure that the throwing area is clear on all sides. (2) Completely clear the impact area (the throwing sector). (3) Retrieve your own implement—javelins should never be thrown back. If there are two or more throwers, all of you should retrieve your javelins at the same time, after everyone has thrown.

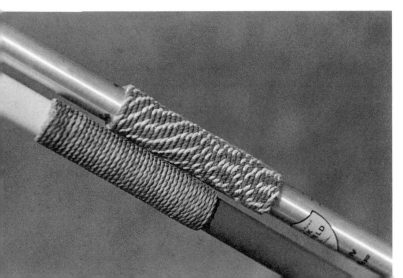

The javelin grip.
The grip on the new javelin (top) is 2 inches forward on the shaft compared to the old (bottom).

The approach runway is 13 feet 1½ inches wide and 98 feet 6 inches to 120 feet long. Throws must be made from behind the scratch-line (arc of a circle) drawn with a radius point 26 feet 3 inches back down the run way. The surface of the throwing area is usually grass or synthetic material.

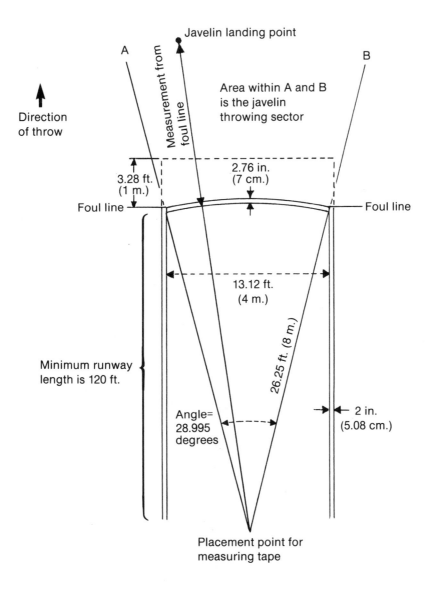

THE BIOMECHANICS
OF THE JAVELIN THROW

In throwing the javelin, a high release speed is obviously a goal, since how far a thrown javelin will travel is determined by its velocity. However, equally crucial is how the speed is applied, which involves many variables.

Angle of attack (also known as *throwing angle* and *angle of release*). This describes the angle between the line of the javelin's release and the ground, or as some have said, the angle between the plane of the javelin and the hand. Over the years, throwers and coaches have discovered that a variation of as little as plus or minus 10 degrees can mean an 8 percent loss in distance. Hand and forearm strength are therefore essential and can, among other things, improve the consistency of your throwing angle.

With a change in the shape of the javelin has come a change in the angle of attack. Throwers using the older, longer-traveling javelins threw the implement at a 28- to 30-degree angle (between the jawline and the cheekbone, with the throwing hand held shoulder high). With the new javelin, throwers are throwing at a 30- to 35-degree angle (between the top of the eyebrow and the hairline, with the throwing hand at shoulder height or above).

Body angle, or angle of force. This is the angle of the body in relation to the ground leading into the throw, and is determined by how far the right foot lands in front of the body's center of mass after the crossover (more on the crossover later). For best efficiency, body angle should be no more than 75 degrees and no less than 80 degrees.

Body angle.
Leading into the throw, this is the angle of the body in relation to the ground. It should be no more than 75 degrees and no less than 80 degrees.

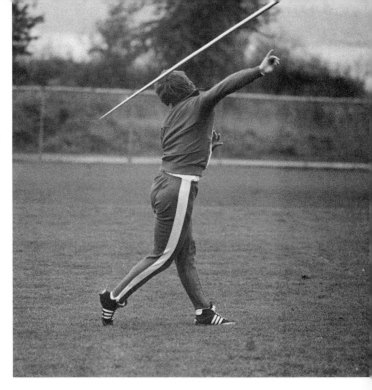

Height of release.
This is determined not only by your body height, but also by your ability to block effectively with your left leg.

Height of release is determined not only by your body height, but also by your ability to block effectively with your left leg. Because of the rise in hard synthetic throwing surfaces, throwers are finding it increasingly difficult to maintain a straight blocking leg when the blocking foot first touches the ground. Why? They simply want to avoid the risk of injury to the knee and back caused by coming down on a synthetic surface with their leg straight. The key to overcoming the problems associated with artificial surfaces, I feel, is to strengthen the legs and back, and also to plant the blocking leg quickly, rather than "drift" onto it (more later).

Vibrations in the javelin as it travels can drastically reduce the distance and stability of its flight. Vibrations are usually the result of a misdirected force angle or the path of the hand not being in line with the angle of the javelin, or both. A proper force angle requires that:

• power is directed into the shaft of the javelin;
• the athlete throws "through the point"—that is, his hand follows through along the same plane as the implement up to, through, and after the moment of release;

- the athlete does not pull down on the javelin at the release point;
- the athlete does not drop the throwing elbow upon achieving the proper throwing angle, but rather keeps the arm straight by raising the throwing shoulder up. This prevents "javelin elbow"—tendinitis of the throwing elbow caused by slinging the javelin with the elbow dropped.

The spin of the javelin, I feel (though most physicists would refute me), can enhance the flight of the javelin by contributing to lift forces and also stabilize the javelin in flight. Good javelin spin should occur naturally if every other aspect of the throw is properly performed.

THE GRIP

In general, the javelin is held diagonally across the palm. When the javelin is held properly, the palm should form a groove for the javelin to lie in. There are three finger grips you can use. In grip #1, the thumb and first finger grip behind the cord. In grip #2, the thumb and second finger grip behind the cord, with the first finger curled or lying straight down the shaft. In grip #3, known as the fork grip, the first and second fingers grip behind the cord.

I prefer the first and second grips because the javelin has less tendency to come off the palm during the throwing motion. At the moment of release, these two grips impart some spin to the javelin. However, the third variation has been used by many successful throwers, notably Duncan Atwood of the University of Washington, a 306-foot thrower with the old javelin and the 1984 and '86 American champion. The problem with this grip? It tends not to impart any spin and to come off the palm during the throw, and it requires a strong hand.

Since the goal in this event is to throw the javelin as far as possible, both speed and accuracy are important. The faster the javelin is moving when it leaves your hand, the farther it will go, provided it is released at the optimum angle. In order for the momentum of your approach run to be transferred efficiently into and through the shaft, the javelin must be aligned with the direction of the throw, as if you were throwing a dart.

While walking or jogging slowly, practice carrying the javelin with your arm raised so the implement is slightly above your ear or head, parallel to the ground or pointed slightly down. The javelin should rest comfortably in your upturned palm.

Gripping the Javelin

Grip #1.
The thumb and first finger grip behind the cord.

Grip #2.
The thumb and second finger grip behind the cord.

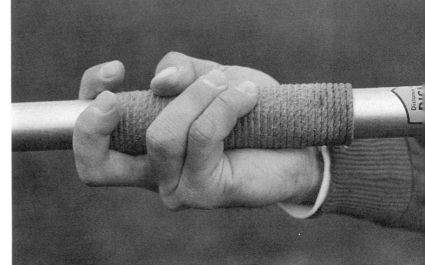

Grip #3.
The fork grip: the first and second fingers grip behind the cord.

GETTING STARTED
IN THE JAVELIN THROW

Listed below are the steps you should go through in order to learn how to throw the javelin if you are a beginner, and to prepare for a successful campaign every season if you are more advanced.

The Standing Weighted-Ball Throw

Often beginners find that throwing the javelin itself is a somewhat difficult matter. Therefore I recommend that the beginner start out by throwing weighted balls into a curtain or net from the standing (power) position. Doing so not only drills proper body mechanics, it also strengthens the shoulder and elbow of the throwing arm. In Seattle there are many fishing stores where we can purchase lead weights in 1-, 2-, 4-, and 6-pound increments. We throw with these weights three times a week in preparation for the precompetitive training season. A typical throwing session will entail throwing each of the four weights a specific number of times until a thrower gradually builds up to 100 throws per session.

A

Standing throws.
Start the standing throw with your weight back, on your right leg, and with the javelin drawn back as shown. Note the position of the lead (left) arm and that the head is up, the shoulder of the throwing arm high (A). Now pull your lead arm across, and pushing off on your right foot, step forward onto your left leg. By pulling your left arm in sharply at the elbow and pushing with your right hip, you assume the bow, or power, position (B). With your right shoulder leading, pull the javelin forward, through the throw. Release the javelin with a snap of the wrist, flipping your palm down (C).

Standing Throws

In addition to being the next step in learning the throwing motion, standing throws are a good warm-up activity for experienced throwers. They are usually done 20 to 30 times in a workout, with the javelin traveling anywhere from 100 feet (for the novice) to 200 feet (for the advanced thrower). Much of your time, in both standing and moving throws, will be spent learning to align the javelin properly. Remember: the javelin should point in the direction it is moving.

Stand sideways to the direction of the throw, with your feet about shoulder width apart. Your left foot points in the direction of the throw while your right foot points slightly to the right of the direction of the throw (at about a 45-degree angle). The throwing arm is extended back as far as possible, and the lead arm is held shoulder high across the chest or out in the direction of the throw. The palm of the throwing hand is up, shoulder high, supporting the javelin.

Your weight is on your back (right) leg and your body is canted slightly back to get maximum comfortable extension of the throwing arm. Your head is up and you should look down the shaft, as if you were sighting down a rifle.

As you pull your lead arm across, your weight starts to shift from the back

B   C

234 leg to the lead leg (that is, you push off your right foot). Your right leg and hip should be pushing as you stretch your chest and torso by pulling your left arm in sharply at the elbow. This is the bow, or power position.

Then, with your right shoulder leading, pull the javelin forward, through the throw. Your throwing elbow should form a right angle with your upper arm, which is shoulder high, and your throwing hand should pass over the elbow, not outside it. Now release the javelin with a snap of the wrist that flips your palm down. Throughout, as a result of the throwing motion, the torso, hips, and right knee all rotate, much as they do for the shot and discus events.

Practice the standing throw until you can really feel the power position. This is what you will be striving for at the end of the momentum-building approach run.

The Crossover and Throw

A crossover step (or steps) is the last part of your approach before a throw, and I recommend performing one or two as part of the learning progression. Start

The crossover and throw.
Stand with your feet shoulder width apart, draw the javelin back as you did for the standing throw, and step forward vigorously with your left foot, in line with your right foot (A). Next, make a crossover step with your right foot as if you were kicking a soccer ball. Your right

A   B

by standing with your feet shoulder width apart and draw the javelin back as you did for the standing throw. Now step forward with your left foot in line with your right foot, and then make a crossover step forward with your right foot as if it were kicking a soccer ball. Your right foot should land at a 45-degree angle to the line of your forward movement. Then move your left foot forward vigorously and plant in the direction of your throw. Push off from your right foot, your right shoulder and elbow coming forward as in the standing throw, and release the javelin. As you'll see when you start doing full approaches, the crossover step positions your body for a forceful, vigorous throw. Remember: Never slow down during this phase.

Once you feel comfortable performing the crossover step-and-throw, you're ready to start adding more steps to your approach and throwing the javelin in earnest.

foot should land at a 45-degree angle to your line of movement (B, C). Step forward vigorously with your left foot, plant in the direction of your throw, and follow through as you did for the standing throw (D, E).

C D E

THROWING THE JAVELIN

The Carry

The over-the-shoulder carry is the most widely used in the javelin throw, perhaps because it's most conducive to a natural running rhythm. The javelin is usually held level with the top of the head. The point of the javelin faces downward to enable you to draw the javelin back and align it properly before the crossover that leads to the throw (more on the crossover in a moment).

The carry.
Using whichever of the three grips is most comfortable for you, start by holding the javelin level with the top of your head, with the point facing down.

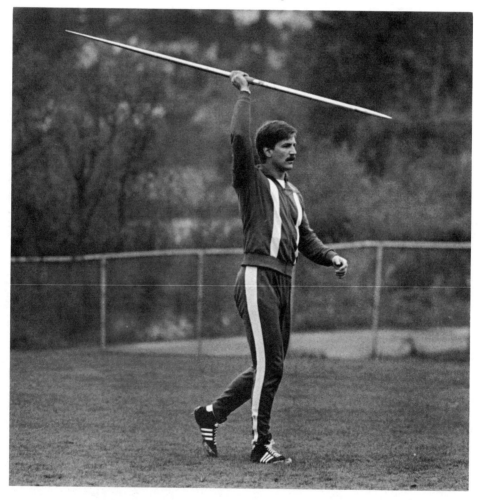

The Approach Run

The approach consists of several parts: a run building to a maximum controllable speed; the draw-back (drawing back the javelin), which occurs upon reaching a predetermined check mark; then two more running steps followed by one or more crossover steps before the actual throw. Beginners will take a 6- to 8-step run while more experienced athletes take anywhere from 10 to 14 steps. See page 52 for the method of setting up a run and putting in check marks.

A good approach run should be made at a controlled speed that can be maintained even through the crossovers. Never make the approach so long that it causes you to be erratic or out of control for the actual throw, and start at a short distance, only lengthening your run when you and your coach feel that you are ready.

The approach run.
Make your approach run of 6 to 14 steps at a controlled speed that you can maintain even through the crossovers.

The Draw-Back

At the University of Washington, we usually use two check marks to mark our approach: one for the starting point, the second for the place to start drawing back the javelin in preparation for the throw. The draw-back should (1) start with the left foot (for the right-handed thrower); (2) take no more than two steps to complete; (3) put the javelin into the desired throwing angle (33 to 35 degrees; and (4) lead into the last crossover steps before the throw.

When you make the draw-back, you should become aware of the point of the javelin, and you should feel as if your body is "running away from" your throwing hand. With the javelin near your head, you should also feel as if you were sighting down a gun barrel, and you should start to establish a distant target for your throw.

The draw-back.
The draw-back (A) begins with a step onto the left foot (if you are a right-handed thrower). It takes no more than two steps to complete (B, C) and leads into the first crossover step (D). Note the angle of the javelin at the end of the draw-back: about 33 to 35 degrees.

A

B

The Crossover

During the crossover you are attempting to position your center of mass ahead of your shoulders in an effort to keep your body weight over the drive (rear) leg and to establish the critical force (body) angle discussed earlier. It is a transition between the run-up and the throw. As a coach, I prefer that the javelin thrower takes only one crossover; however, this varies from individual to individual, with novice throwers taking four, five, or even six crossovers before the throw. Duncan Atwood uses two, sometimes three, crossovers before he releases the javelin. The key is controlling your speed into the final crossover before release, and my point is that if you use only one, you are less likely to slow down. Cary Feldman was extremely adept at maintaining speed by using only one crossover, whereas another University of Washington thrower, Rod

C

D

240   Ewaliko, could actually increase his tempo by using more than one.

The mechanics of the crossover for a right-handed thrower are as follows (a left-hander should mirror these techniques):

1. The step with the left leg that precedes the final drive of the right leg is important because it sets up the momentum and tempo of the throw. To make this step work, plant the left foot forward, in line with the path of the right foot. With that step, the legs should be rather widely separated, and the hips and shoulders should be parallel to the javelin. This enables an aggressive swing of the right leg into the final crossover.

2. Now we come to the actual crossover. The right leg's cross step is similar in motion to a soccer kick, in that the right leg sweeps past the left leg, with the right foot angled outward slightly. The right arm has drawn the javelin back, and the left arm now swings across the body (how far depends on the individual), with the palm of the left hand facing the direction of the throw, thumb down.

3. The action of the crossing leg should be forward and down, with the knee and foot leading the way. The action of the left arm prevents the right hip

The crossover.

The crossover begins with the left foot stepping in line with the right foot. With that step, your legs are rather widely separated, and your hips and shoulders are parallel to the javelin (A). Now comes the actual crossover step, with the right leg sweeping past the left and the right foot angled out slightly. The right arm has drawn the javelin back and the left arm now swings across the body with the palm of the left hand facing in the direction of the throw (B, C).

A   B   C

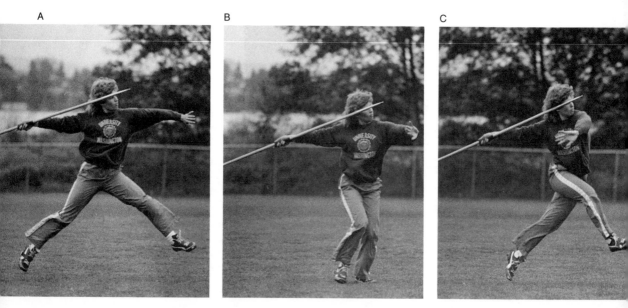

from rotating forward completely. Your right foot should strike the ground firmly, as a triple jumper's would, at a 45-degree angle to your forward direction.

4. Now drive explosively off your trailing left leg, in sync with the forward thrust of your right leg. Doing so helps pull your hips and lower body ahead of your shoulders, propelling you into the power position. If you drive correctly off your left foot, you should assume the power position naturally.

241

The Delivery, or Throw

During the throw you push off the right foot after driving the left ahead; sweep the left arm, elbow up, in front of you and then down (remember, you have cocked your left arm more or less across your chest during the crossover); and plant the left foot in the direction of the throw. Do not drift forward, *drive* forward, so that the right arm's throwing motion is initiated through the body and legs.

Your right foot should strike the ground firmly, landing at about a 45-degree angle to the direction of the throw (D). Driving forward explosively with your left leg puts you in position for the actual throw (E).

D   E

A   B

The delivery, or throw.

To initiate the throw after driving the left leg forward, push off with the right foot and sweep the left arm up and in front of you (A). Keep the javelin close to your head until your shoulders are square with the direction of the throw. As the left arm sweeps down, pull the throwing shoulder forward, and then pull forward with the throwing arm, your elbow leading (B). Note how the left leg straightens as the body goes over it into the throw. Now the hand snaps forward with maximum acceleration, releasing the javelin (C, D).

Keep the javelin close to your head until your shoulders are square with the direction of your throw. Pull the throwing shoulder forward, and then pull forward with the throwing arm, your elbow leading. This is called *arm strike*. Do not let your hand pass ahead of your elbow—at least not yet. The hand, which is the last part of the arm to move on the throw, is snapped forward with maximum acceleration. A good snapping action cannot occur unless your left (blocking) leg straightens into the throw as your body passes over it. The right elbow leads the javelin through the release until the last moment, and the follow-through and recovery are on the right foot. To avoid fouling, your plant (left) foot should come down before the throw at least 6 to 8 feet from the foul line. By doing so you can drive forward after releasing the javelin and not be

C

D

forced to stop your forward momentum too suddenly. To some, stopping so far back from the line may seem to be sacrificing throwing distance, but believe me, if your throwing technique is correct, you'll actually gain distance by being able to follow through comfortably.

Remember, the angle of attack, or release, should be between 30 and 35 degrees (between the top of your eyebrow and your hairline), and your body angle in the power position should be between 75 and 80 degrees. Wind direction and wind speed will cause you to alter your angle of throw at times; only through practice and experiencing different wind conditions will you know which angles work best for which conditions.

Putting It All Together: The Javelin

Review the instructions on the preceding pages and study this photo sequence to help refine your javelin-throwing technique.

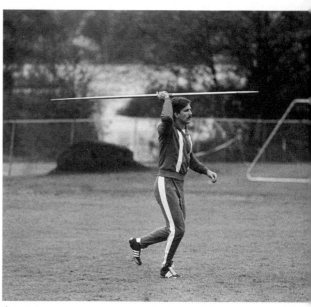

A

The carry and approach run (A, B).

D

E

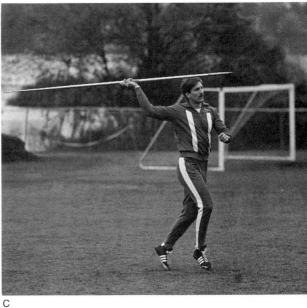

B

C

The draw-back (C, D, E, F).

The crossover (here, two crossover steps are performed) (G, H, I, J, K).

F

G

(continued)

H

I

The delivery, or throw (L, M, N).

L

M

J

K

The recovery (O).

N

O

OTHER DRILLS AND EXERCISES

The rhythms of different *plyometric exercises,* such as bounding and triple jumping, parallel the rhythms of the javelin throw, especially during the draw-back and crossover phases. Plyometrics can also build upper and lower body elasticity, explosiveness, and strength.

Kar-i-o-ka drills, with the javelin drawn back and held steady while you run sideways, your right leg swinging in front of the left and your hips rotating back and forth, are especially helpful for learning balance and developing your crossover step.

Practicing a *series of crossovers,* in sets of 40 yards each, can improve your javelin alignment, the force of your foot on landing, your body angle, and your footwork for this tricky maneuver.

Running with the javelin in the overhead-carry position can help you overcome the awkwardness of this running style.

Elbow Exercises

A strong throwing elbow is essential if you're going to be successful in the javelin throw. Some of the more popular elbow exercises are:

- Throwing weighted balls (in my estimation the best exercise).
- Bent-arm pullovers with a barbell or E-Z Curl bar.
- French curls with a barbell or E-Z Curl bar.
- Wrist and forearm curls with a barbell or E-Z Curl bar.
- Chopping exercises with a sledgehammer, splitting maul, or ax.
- Javelin stretching exercises (see illustrations).
- The javelin towel drill (see illustrations).

COACHING TIPS
FOR THE JAVELIN THROW

- The crossover steps are similar in tempo to the bounding motions used in the triple jump (see page 133).
- Remind the athlete to attain his focal point early, during the draw-back phase of the throw. He should sight down the javelin as if sighting down a gun barrel.

• Watch to make sure the thrower does not slow his run during the crossover phase. He should maintain his speed and move very comfortably into and through the crossovers.

• Remember: the thrower's hips and throwing shoulder should be parallel to the javelin at the start of the power position.

• The thrower should start his throw as soon as his right foot makes contact with the ground during the last crossover (when the right foot pushes off onto the left foot and the free arm moves across the body).

• Stress to your thrower that he should never lose sight of the focal point until the javelin has left his hand.

The Hammer Throw

It's a shame that one of the most exciting and exhilarating events in track and field, not only from the spectator's standpoint but from the athlete's as well, is allowed to be performed at the high school level in only two states, New Hampshire and Rhode Island. For that matter, until recently not many junior colleges have thrown the hammer either. Thanks to coaching clinics, lectures, and other efforts by Stewart Togher, a Scottish coach brought to the United States by The Athletics Congress (TAC), this bleak and often frustrating situation is changing. Interest in the hammer throw is developing throughout the nation, especially on the West Coast. This is also due in part to the many training venues developed for the 1984 Olympic Games, and to many of the junior colleges, especially in California, that have included the hammer in their state championships. However, we still have a long way to go if we are to attract the many talented young men in this country who could throw the hammer (so far, a male-only event). It would be a coach's dream, for instance, to be able to train all the professional middle linebackers in football for the hammer! At our school *all* throwers, javelin included, try the hammer.

THE IMPLEMENT

Like the other throwing implements (the javelin especially), the hammer must conform to a strict set of specifications, and like the shot put, it is thrown from a 7-foot circle. The hammer itself consists of three parts: the head, the wire, and the grip, or handle.

The hammer head, sometimes called the ball, is spherical and made of iron or other metals harder than brass. The head may be solid, or it may be hollow

Though once limited to college-level and elite competitors, the hammer throw is beginning to gain interest at the junior college and high school level as well.

to allow filling (usually lead pellets), but the filling must be inserted in such a manner that the center of gravity is not more than 6 millimeters (0.236 inch) from the center of the sphere.

The wire is a single straight length of spring steel wire not less than 3 millimeters (0.118 inch) in diameter. The wire is looped at both ends for attachment to the hammer head and the grip.

The grip may be of either single- or double-loop construction and is rigid (without hinged joints) to prevent any appreciable stretching during the course of the throw. The grip is attached to the wire in a fashion that will prevent any increase in the overall length of the hammer when it is swung. The other end of the wire is attached to the hammer head by means of a swivel, either plain or ball-bearing, imbedded into the hammer. A swivel may not be used to attach the wire to the grip.

The weight of the hammer varies depending on age classification. Junior-class athletes (high school) in this country throw a 12-pound hammer, whereas some foreign countries will use a 14-pound hammer. College and open throwers use a sixteen-pound implement.

The minimum overall length of the hammer is 3 feet 10¼ inches; the maximum is 3 feet 11¾ inches. The hammer head is from 4.33 to 5.118 inches in diameter.

The object of the event is to see who can throw the hammer farthest within a 40 degree-wide throwing zone. The rules of competition are restrictive, determined mainly by safety concerns for both athlete and spectator. The hammer is thrown within the confines of a chain-link cage with an opening only large enough to accommodate the throw. There are no restrictions on the positions and actions of the thrower. A competitor may, for instance, interrupt an attempted throw and start again.

The thrower may use a glove to protect the hand that holds the handle, but the finger ends of the glove must be open, and the glove must be smooth on the back and front. An additional layer of leather may be attached to the palm of the glove for further protection, but despite these precautions, the throwing hand can still take a beating because of the great centrifugal force generated by the turns. For this reason, competitors are allowed to tape each finger of the handle-holding hand individually.

A competitor is also allowed to lay the hammer head on the ground, inside or outside the circle prior to commencing his preliminary winds (turns).

It is not considered to be a foul throw if the hammer head touches the surface of the ring during the preliminary winds and turns or even during the throw itself. It is not considered to be a foul if the hammer strikes the cage upon

Never throw the hammer without a protective leather glove. By the rules of competition, the finger ends of the glove must be open, but you may attach an additional layer of leather to the glove's palm.

release and lands within the throwing sector, an area extending outward at a 40-degree angle from the center of the ring. It is a foul if the ball lands outside the sector, or outside the ring itself after the release.

As in the other field events, once a competitor has been called by an official, he has 90 seconds to complete a throw. Therefore, in the course of the throw and if he has not committed a foul, the thrower may stop, lay the implement down, and return to a starting position.

THE BIOMECHANICS OF THE HAMMER THROW

As we shall see, the hammer is a sprinting event in a way. To throw the hammer efficiently, you must have quick feet, a good sense of balance, and most important, the willingness to "run with the hammer head"—that is, to relax and move with the hammer rather than fight it. This is probably *the* most important concept you can learn as a hammer thrower, because it is completely contrary to what is taught in the shot and the discus. For example, a discus thrower tries to stay ahead of the implement by "dragging" it into the center of the ring. With a hammer, this just can't be done. You will be spinning with the hammer, using your body as the axis of the spin. You must keep up with the hammer's orbit. You must not give in to the mind's concern for self-preservation by "baling out" when the hammer attains terrific horizontal speed.

Like the other throwing events, the hammer has its own rhythm, for which leg and back strength is more important than upper body strength. Most elite hammer throwers can squat at least 500 pounds and clean 300 pounds. They are usually satisfied with a 300-pound bench press.

Generally speaking, the throwing motion may be described as a rotational one (horizontal velocity around a vertical axis), moving counterclockwise for a right-handed thrower, and pivoting alternately on the heel and toe of the left foot from the back to the front of the ring. The thrower also pivots on the ball of the right foot as the hammer head passes in front of him, thereby allowing the body to continue its rotating, forward-moving "run with the hammer." Usually three rotations are performed, four if the thrower conducts the first turn on the ball of the left foot. Like the other throwing events, the distance achieved in the throw depends on the velocity and the angle (optimally 42 degrees) at which the hammer is delivered.

Before discussing the "how to's" of the hammer throw, let's look at some basic concepts.

Hammer and thrower share a common *center of mass* during the turns. This is where my concept of the hammer throw has changed drastically. During Scott Neilson's time as an undergraduate at the University of Washington, we taught our hammer throwers to try to lead, or stay ahead of, the hammer head at the onset of each turn. In other words we wanted the thrower's front hip to lead his trunk and shoulders, and thereby his entire body would lead the hammer.

Now the concept, as practiced by the Russians and the current U.S. champion, Judd Logan, is to maintain a longer support phase (where the knees are bent in a kind of sitting position—more later) with both feet at the onset of each turn. In all turns we strive to rotate 90 degrees to the left, with both feet in contact with the surface of the ring, thereby establishing the proper relationship between hammer and thrower, where the hammer rotates and not the body. (More on this later.)

The thrower should try to establish a *long radius* (the distance between the vertical axis—the body—and the hammer head) during the turns to make the hammer head move faster. You do this by extending your arms.

Countering (sitting and leaning back as you rotate the hammer) can effectively create up to 700 pounds of pull in a 16-pound hammer. That is, centrifugal (outward) force can increase the apparent weight of the hammer up to 700 pounds. This pull, in turn, creates a longer radius and more speed (the hammer head moves faster).

Linear velocity refers to the hammer head's speed as it is rotated, and a high linear velocity is desirable in order to ensure a long throw. High linear velocities are attained by means of a rapid rotation of the athlete and hammer.

It takes many months of practice to attain a long radius and good turning speed for a high linear velocity. So often, throwers will shorten their radius as the turn speed increases, thus decreasing the hammer's linear velocity; or they will slow down as they strive to reach for a longer radius, again causing the hammer head to slow down. (A long radius requires straight arms, which is difficult to learn because of a natural tendency to pull in on the hammer by bending the elbows as speed increases.)

Vertical posture refers to keeping the hips (center of mass) directly under the thrower, while maintaining a straight, flat back. On the double-support phase of each turn (more later), the hips should feel as if they are pushed forward.

The *duration* of the *double support phase* and how it is applied during the wind-up is critical. During this phase, the thrower sits back on the ball of his right foot (vertical posture) and pivots on the heel of his left foot, maintaining perfect coordination between himself and the hammer (the shoulders and the pelvis are in the same plane). Throughout every turn the thrower must rotate 90 degrees to the left before the right foot is picked up. (This is where discus throwers have trouble learning hammer technique, because you can "drag" the discus behind you, but not the hammer. Why is this so? Mainly because the amazing amount of centrifugal force the hammer attains can dramatically exceed the thrower's weight.) A successful thrower appears to be totally relaxed, or as Banderchuk says, "giving back" to the hammer, all the way up to the moment he crosses to the high point of rotation (more later).

The *single-support phase* (more later) on the left foot should be very brief as the thrower progresses across the ring. It occurs after the thrower has rotated 90 degrees to the left during the double-support phase and ends after the right foot makes contact with the circle at the high point of rotation. During this phase the thrower is passive: going with the hammer, and not making any active movements with his pelvic girdle or legs.

Leading the hammer occurs only after passing the high point. The thrower begins to actively rotate himself around his supporting right leg and foot and strives to begin an immediate active action on the hammer. During the single-support phase the thrower "runs with the hammer," but during this phase, the thrower tries to "run ahead" of the hammer with his entire body, except his arms. During this "running action," the thrower feels the continuous pull of the hammer through the arms to his shoulders.

By shortening the duration of the single-support phase and lengthening the double-support phase, it is possible to increase the speed of the hammer. In other words, the thrower's body develops greater rotational speed than the hammer head only at the end of the single-support phase. The sooner the right foot reestablishes contact with the ground after the single-support phase, the greater the acceleration path of the hammer head. It means lifting the right foot from the surface incredibly quickly and replacing it just as quickly; otherwise the hammer will "run away" from the thrower.

By lengthening this phase of each turn, the thrower has a better chance of correctly maintaining his *vertical axis of rotation.* An improper vertical axis is a common fault in throwers until they learn all aspects of the double-support technique.

As a coach, you should not make your final selection of hammer throwers until you have had a chance to experiment and observe athletes performing various hammer drills. Can the prospective thrower adapt to a heel-toe movement across the circle? Can he learn to "run" with the hammer? Once an athlete demonstrates that he can throw the hammer with reasonable success and that he wants to get serious about the event, he must start developing his lower body strength. Again, a long throwing radius is not the product of dominant upper body strength! Countering the hammer's massive pull requires lower back, hip, and leg strength. Weight training and contests among hammer throwers should be conducted, therefore, in the squat, the clean, and the snatch. Instead of the bench press, the hammer thrower should do the dead lift; instead of curls, he should do shoulder shrugs—all those exercises that improve total-body strength or strength in the back, hips, and legs.

GETTING STARTED
IN THE HAMMER THROW

Learning how to hold the hammer, how to set it in motion by swinging (winding) it over your head, how to move from the back to the front of the ring by pivoting on the heel and toe of your left foot (if you're a right-handed thrower), are just some of the things you should first learn as a beginning thrower. You should practice these skills every day as part of your warm-up before weight training, plyometrics, or actual throwing. A word of caution, however: Perhaps more than any other throwing implement, the hammer in the wrong set of hands is a dangerous weapon. You should practice all phases of the event either in the throwing cage or in an extremely open field, with no one—repeat, *no one*—anywhere near you.

Gripping the Hammer

Hold the hammer in both hands, with the handle resting on the middle of the fingers of the left hand, which is the one you should glove. Wrap the fingers of the right hand over the left to provide a secure and stable grip.

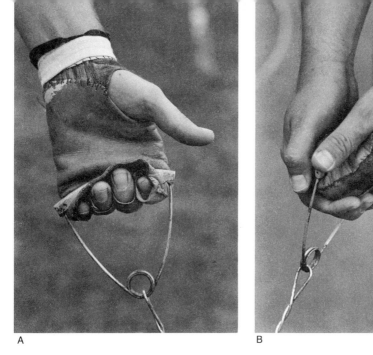

A   B

Gripping the hammer.
The handle rests in the middle of the fingers of the left (glove) hand (A). The fingers of the right hand wrap over the left for a more secure grip (B).

Swinging the Hammer

Setting the hammer in motion initially requires swinging it around your head without moving your feet. This is called the *swing phase* of the event, and swings are often referred to by throwers as *winds.* To perform swings successfully, you should have great flexibility in your trunk and shoulders—another reason for developing only moderate upper body strength. Swings (1) set the rhythm and speed by which you enter the first turn; (2) set the path or angle of the hammer head into the first turn (where you begin the footwork that starts you from the back to the front of the ring); (3) set the high and low points of the hammer path (the hammer swings in an orbit diagonal to the ground, not horizontal to it); (4) help you establish your balance (remember, your body is the vertical axis around which the hammer rotates) prior to your entry into the first turn; and (5) help establish the length of the radius during the turns.

Most throwers take two preliminary swings before starting to pivot toward the front of the ring into what is called the *turn phase.* There are many, many ways to start the swing phase. To get the feel for swinging the hammer properly, stand erect, facing the back of the ring, with your back straight, eyes level, and

Swinging the Hammer

A   B   C

G   H   I

To initiate the swing phase of the hammer throw, wherein you swing the hammer around your head without moving your feet, stand erect facing the back of the ring (A), and gripping the hammer properly, set it in motion by first rocking it back somewhat clockwise (B), then bringing it forward counterclockwise (C), which is the direction in which you will make it swing. Use your arms now to keep the hammer moving counterclockwise around you (D). The high point of the hammer's first orbit should be above and behind your left shoulder

(E). After traveling behind you (F,G), the hammer should reach its low point 45 degrees to the right of your body (H). On the second orbit, keep your head high (I, J), and as the hammer passes to a point over your right shoulder, reach back with your hands and arms to create a longer path (K). As the hammer completes its second orbit, you would normally prepare to go into the turn phase of the throw, but when starting out, just practice the swings, or winds, in isolation.

head steady. As in the shot put and the discus, your back is facing the direction of the throw, and your feet are shoulder width apart. Holding the hammer as described, set it in motion by swinging it counterclockwise around yourself if you're a right-handed thrower, clockwise if you're a lefty. On the first wind the low point of the hammer is 45 degrees to the right of your body, and the high point is above and behind your left shoulder. Keep your head held high. As the hammer head passes to a point over your right shoulder, reach back with your hands and arms toward the hammer to create a longer path. Do not apply too much force to your swing; just smoothly and deliberately swing the hammer around your head two or three times, then stop by lowering the head to the ground during the low phase of its orbit. Repeat 8 to 10 times per practice session. Practice for a week before attempting a full-scale throw.

The Walk-and-Wind Drill

Once you feel comfortable performing winds, try executing them while walking forward. You'll discover a rhythm for stepping with either foot: the hammer will be behind and to your left as you step with your right foot, behind and to your right as you step with your left. Repeat for a total of 8 to 10 steps. Rest. Repeat for 3 to 6 sets.

The Standing Throw

The next step in your progression toward throwing the hammer is to practice the standing throw.

Stand at the front of the ring, perpendicular to the direction of your throw and with your left foot closest to the front perimeter if you are a right-handed thrower (as always, mirror the directions if you are a lefty). Grip the hammer as described and make two counterclockwise swings with it. At the end of the second swing, release the hammer in one continuous sweeping motion. Your arms should finish high and to the left, with your right arm almost over your head. Repeat 8 to 10 times. Practice this drill for a week before attempting a full-scale throw. If it feels awkward at first, try throwing a rigid implement such as a sledgehammer, or shorten your wire by double-looping it through the handle and the swivel.

Learning to Heel-and-Toe

If you study the footwork of accomplished hammer throwers, you'll see that they progress from the back to the front of the ring by pivoting mainly on the heel and toe of their left foot.

An excellent way to learn the choreography of the hammer throw is to practice the following drill:

Standing at the back of the ring, facing away from the direction you normally would throw, lay a sturdy 5- to 6-foot-long dowel across your shoulders and drape your wrists over each end. Now start the footwork of the throw by pivoting outward on the heel of your left foot until the foot is at a 90-degree angle to your right foot; then lift your right foot off the ring surface and swing it in front of your left. Do not swing the right leg wide; rather, keep it close to the left leg. As your right foot makes its swing, your left foot will naturally shift its pivot point from the heel to the toe (actually the ball of the foot, which should be flat as your weight comes onto it). When you plant your right foot next to the left, you should have made approximately a 270-degree turn from your starting point; in other words, if the back of the ring is South and the front of the ring is North, you should now be facing West. Don't stop there, though! Complete the pivot on the ball of your left and right feet. Then, just as you did when you started, pivot out on your left heel until you are nearly facing East, bring your right foot around and close to the left, and see where you end up when your feet are once again aligned.

Normally, hammer throwers go through three such heel-and-toe pivots before releasing the hammer with their bodies nearly perpendicular to the front of the ring. As you'll note when you practice the steps, there are periods during these rotations when both feet are on the ground and supporting the thrower (the *double-support phase*) and other periods when only the left foot is supporting the thrower while the right foot makes its swing (the *single-support phase*).

The Turn Drill

Now it's time to get a better feel for the centrifugal forces that turning the hammer can develop.

Properly gripping the hammer while standing on the grass or in the middle of the throwing ring, start it in motion by using your body as the central axis and pivoting around a central point. Your back and arms should be straight, your legs slightly flexed, and you should strive to "run with the hammer," that

Learning to Heel-and-Toe

A

B

C

G

H

I

D   E   F

J

Holding a sturdy pole across your shoulders as shown, face toward the back of the ring (A). Now begin the heel-and-toe action by pivoting outward on the heel of your left foot until it is at a 90-degree angle to your right foot (B). Then lift your right foot off the ring surface, and keeping your right leg close to the left, swing your right foot in front of the left (C). As you do so, the weight on your left foot will automatically shift from the heel to the ball. Plant your right foot forward of the left (D). Continue the left foot's pivot on its ball (E). Once the left foot is at a 90-degree angle to the right, pivot again on the left heel (F). Lift your right foot off the ring (G). Swing it around (H). Plant it (I, J). Keep pivoting in this fashion to the front of the ring.

is, keep it right in front of you. Do four or five turns. Stop. Regain your equilibrium. Repeat 6 to 8 times.

You can also perform the turn drill using a rigid implement, such as a sledgehammer, and you can try it using only your left hand. Be careful though: at all times maintain a good grip on the hammer.

The Heel-and-Toe-with-Hammer Drill

Once you know how to heel-and-toe without the hammer, and once you've gotten a feel for "running" with the hammer, it's time to combine the two. Your first attempts at doing so should be with a lightweight training hammer or with a rigid implement such as a sledgehammer, holding it by the end of the handle. Concentrate first on the movement of your feet, second on the position of your arms and upper body.

Starting in the back of the ring and facing away from the mouth of the cage, grip the hammer, set it in motion with a couple of counterclockwise winds, and near the end of the second one, make your outward, counterclock-

The heel-and-toe-with-hammer drill. In this drill, you "run" with the hammer as you did for the turn drill, and heel-and-toe as you did when shouldering the pole.

wise pivot on the heel of your left foot. Try to keep the hammer in front of you as you cross with your right foot and make your series of pivots all the way to the front of the ring. Note how both you and the hammer accelerate as you make your progress from the back to the front. There is no room in this event for slowing down—once you begin your turns and heel-and-toe work, you are on your way in an ever accelerating movement across the ring.

At the front of the ring, let your arms down to bring the hammer to a stop. Be prepared to keep "running" with it until it stops completely.

Now return to the back of the ring and try the technique again. Try to resist the temptation to draw your arms in and thus slow the hammer's momentum. Instead keep your feet moving and your chest even with the hammer head. Also, as you perform your winds at the beginning of the drill, try to make your second wind faster than your first, so that you accelerate into your first full-body turn. Again, acceleration and smooth, quick footwork are key. Repeat 8 to 10 times.

Practice these drills daily for a solid week. Only when you feel comfortable performing each are you ready to put them all together and throw the hammer.

THE HAMMER-THROW TECHNIQUE

The Grip and the Winds

As you did for many of the earlier drills, assume the "ready" position in the back of the ring: your back straight and facing the direction of your throw, your hands gripping the handle, your feet shoulder width apart. Set the hammer in motion, using two counterclockwise winds. Remember: On the first wind, the low point is 45 degrees to the right of your body, the high point is above and behind your left shoulder. Keep your head high. As the hammer head passes to a point behind the right shoulder, "reach back" for it with both arms.

The Transition from the Last Wind to the First Turn

The transition into the first turn, wherein your body becomes a rotating axis for the hammer, begins as the hammer descends after its second wind. The second wind should be faster than the first—it sets the rhythm for the turn, or rotation, phase of the event.

As the hammer makes its second descent, turn your left foot outward by pivoting on your left heel, just as you did for the Heel-and-Toe-with-Hammer drill. Cross your right foot over your left, feel the pivot switch from your left heel to your left toe to your left heel again, as you repeat the movement and enter the first turn. Remember to pivot onto the ball of your right foot as you return to the double-support phase.

There are a few important things to remember as you make the transition from the last wind to the first turn, and then as you go into subsequent turns:

1. There is a definite increase in tempo as you start the first turn, and the tempo only increases with each subsequent turn, until you finish with an explosive release at the front of the ring.

2. At the end of the second wind (as you begin the outward pivot on the heel of the left foot), your weight is actually on your pivoting right foot. Then, as you move the hammer head forcefully to the left, your weight shifts to the ball of your left foot and your right leg can begin its swing around the left as it pivots.

3. During the first turn, strive to keep your trunk erect; then lower your center of mass (by flexing your knees) on each turn thereafter. The flexing should occur when both feet are on the ground (that is, during the double-

support phase), and you'll find that, as well, you'll want to sit back slightly on your right foot. This is known as *countering* the centrifugal force of the hammer, and it's essential if you're not to be pulled off balance.

4. The angle of the hammer to the ground naturally becomes steeper with each turn, until by the last turn it is at a 40- to 42-degree angle.

5. During the turns, try to focus on the hammer head, except when you are moving from the single-support to the double-support phase. Then concentrate on your footwork.

6. Step *across* your left foot with your right foot. Keep your right foot at sock level with your left and close to the left ankle and calf. Sprint, or lead, with the right foot. *Drive* it around and into position; don't just let it hang there while you pivot on your left.

7. On the second turn, and on every turn thereafter, the low point of the hammer head should be in front of you when you are facing the back of the ring, and the high point in front of you when you are facing the direction of the throw. This determines the optimum angle of release.

The Final Turns and the Release

Most accomplished throwers make three turns, releasing the hammer at its high point during the third turn. If your footwork has been correct, and if you have stayed with the hammer, you should be more or less perpendicular to the front of the ring at the moment of release, with your body exploding upward with the hammer. Coming out of the last turn leading to this moment, your hips and knees are flexed. Now as you explode upward, your hips and legs straighten, lifting you upward as well as forward. Your hips are well ahead of your shoulders, but their lifting, rotational movement is synchronized with the movement of the hammer. In all, you should strive for a coordinated unwinding of the knees, hips, and trunk. Your arms should be relaxed and extended—not pulled in—and you should release your grip on the hammer just as it accelerates forward. Follow through, with arms high and to the left, as you did for the standing throw. To avoid fouling, lock your hips and left leg, then lower your torso (center of mass).

Note that the moment of release occurs with the weight shifting from the right to the left foot—just as it does, ultimately, when throwing any object right-handed.

Throwing the Hammer

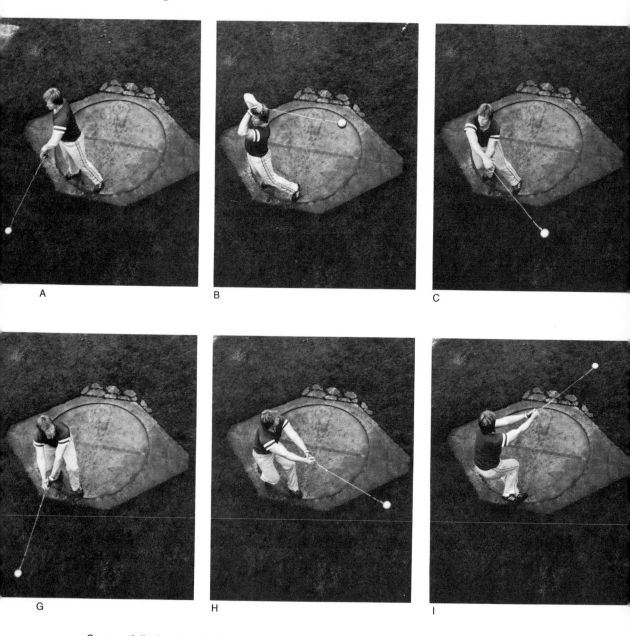

A

B

C

G

H

I

Successfully throwing the hammer begins with assuming an erect stance at the back of the ring, gripping the handle properly, and setting the hammer in motion for the wind phase (A). As you make the two winds, your feet remain planted shoulder width apart and your arms extend, reaching back when the hammer is at its high point over your left shoulder and down and forward when it is at its low point just off your right hip (B, C, D, E, F, G, H). The finish

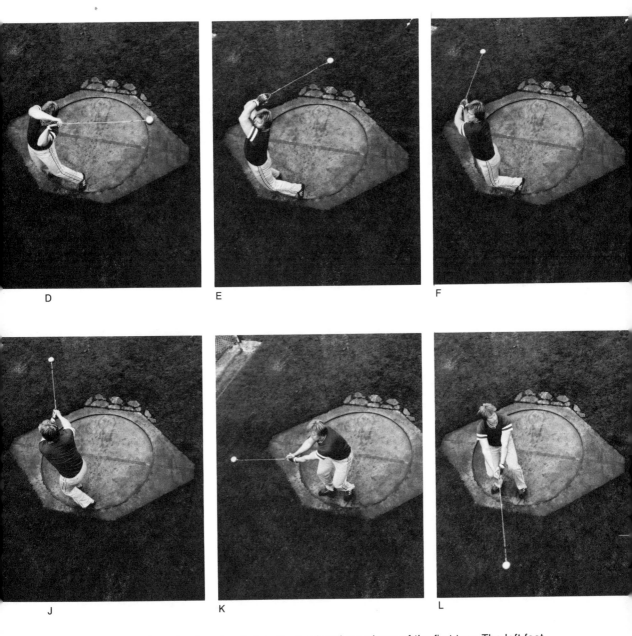

D   E   F

J   K   L

of the wind phase leads naturally into the heel-and-toe phase of the first turn. The left foot pivots outward on its heel, and the right foot swings in a tight arc in front of the left. When the right foot plants, forward of the left, the pivot continues on the ball of the left foot. At the end of the first turn, your weight is evenly balanced over both feet (I, J, K, L, M). But

(continued)

M

N

O

S

T

U

don't stop there! Keep the left foot's heel-and-toe action going into the second turn (N, O, P), and the third (Q, R, S), and if you need it in order to get your body perpendicular to the front edge of the ring, the fourth (T, U). Release the hammer at its high point during your last turn. Coming out of this turn, your hips and knees are flexed, and you explode upward,

P

Q

R

V

W

X

straightening your legs and moving toward the moment of release with a synchronized unwinding of the knees, hips, and trunk. Your arms are relaxed and extended, and you release your grip on the hammer as it accelerates forward. Now follow through, with your arms high and to the left (V, W, X). Congratulations—another perfect throw!

ADDITIONAL DRILLS

• Practice throwing with a 35-pound weight with a short wire. Keep a good, flat, diagonal orbit, with the hammer head up at the high point. Don't let it drop.

• Using two hammers, one in each hand, at 90-degree angles from the body, do the Turn Drill described on page 261. With two hammers, you can also practice rotating from the heel to the toe of your left foot, and crossing over with your right (keep your thumbs up, chest out); and you can learn to pivot on the ball of your right foot. Do the Turn Drill while concentrating on moving the balls of your feet up and down, thereby improving your heel-toe technique.

• Using one hammer, walk around counterclockwise, using the heel-toe technique, to start the hammer rotating. Emphasize countering—sitting back on the right foot when you reenter the double-support phase of the footwork.

TRAINING FOR THE HAMMER THROW

Training for the hammer is as unique as preparing to throw the javelin. Effectiveness in both events requires specific training. In the shot and discus, there are enough parallels that training for one event can promote excellence in the other. Not so in the javelin and hammer. You can do other throwing events, but to excel as a hammer thrower you must train as a hammer thrower!

Strength and size (body weight) are certainly advantageous to successful hammer throwers, and obviously both of these qualities can be dramatically enhanced through weight training. But once again, exercises that are specific for the hammer throw must be given primary consideration. These include squats (front and back), pulls, twists (seated with barbell), snatches, cleans, dead lifts, and side bends. Try to incorporate these exercises into your regular weight training workouts.

Additional exercises include:

• *35-pound plate winds*—pendulum motion (let it swing up, do not pull up), sets of 6 each side. (You can also do turns with this exercise.)

• *Sit backs* (double-support position) with wall pulley or surgical tubing, set of 6.

• *Leg lunges*—back straight, hips out, step out to a back knee drop. Alternate each side for a set of 6 by pushing back to starting position.

• *Split snatch* with a dumbbell. Swing up from the floor—do not drop under as in the conventional snatch exercise.

As we discussed earlier, the rotational forces exerted in the hammer are exceptional. Your rotational speed can be improved by developing your physical strength and practicing your technique. Doing both will allow you to increase the hammer's rotational speed and help you withstand the centrifugal forces that such increased speeds create. Short sprints can help improve foot speed, but a perhaps more effective way to develop foot speed is to train with light or short hammers. These can be rotated more quickly than a conventional hammer, forcing you to move your feet faster during the turn and release phases.

Flexibility and agility are important for all the throws, but in the hammer they are crucial, especially in the shoulders and trunk. Besides doing trunk twists with a barbell, try doing back bends, hand hangs from the horizontal bar, ring work, and certain floor exercises such as the hurdler's stretch and cartwheels. All promote greater flexibility, and thus a longer radius and more speed to the hammer.

If you are a beginner at the hammer throw, you should only do technique work that enables you to establish correct foot and body movements. Your main objective should simply be to make the hammer fly, and your training should reflect this simple and direct approach. Concentration is the key, but remember: when you become tired or confused, frustration can set in. Throwing three times a week, 20 throws per training session, is plenty for a beginner.

If you are an advanced thrower, throwing at least once a week in the off-season, perhaps with a heavier implement, and three to seven days per week in the precompetitive and competitive phases, is a must if you are to approach your maximum potential in the event. An example of training programs for each level might be as follows:

Beginner

1. Five to 10 throws with one, two, and three turns. Work on maintaining relaxed shoulders and arms; learn to sit back on the double-support phase; strive for balance and footwork in order to "run" successfully with the hammer head.

2. Technique work on winds and turns every day. To make an effective

transition from the last wind into the first turn, work on moving the hammer head hard to the left. Work on the transition from the first turn to the second turn, focusing on footwork, arm radius, and release.

3. Speed and agility work twice weekly.

4. Weight training three times weekly.

Advanced

1. Basic technique work as described for the beginner.

2. Concentrate on two to four technical points in each practice. For example: Sets of 5 throws emphasizing arm radius, countering at the high and low points, maintaining the double support for 90 degrees to the left, and when and how to run away from the ball. Work on the release.

3. Ten to 20 light hammer throws, two to three times a week.

4. Continued technique work on only one weak point per practice.

COACHING TIPS
FOR THE HAMMER THROW

• In a way, your thrower's first turn should be like a wind; that is, he should make an easy transition from the wind into the turn.

• The thrower should start his second turn as the right foot makes contact with the ground.

• Stress to your thrower that he should learn, in effect, to walk backward—*lean back!*

• The thrower should learn to counter on his right foot, noting how the speed of the hammer accelerates when he does so.

• In teaching footwork, stress that the thrower should give on the left foot, rise on the right foot.

• He should also pivot on the left foot, not "load it up." Keep it moving.

• Watch that, on the start of the second turn, the thrower has the hammer head directly in front of him.

• The thrower's feet and the hammer move together. The body stays in one system!

• Watch that, on the start of the second wind, the thrower twists his hands and right foot simultaneously. This should happen naturally, with the hands twisting as the thrower reaches back.

• The athlete's toes always face the hammer head; he should let the ball "run." In the double-support phases he should sit back, as if sitting on a chair.

• On the second and subsequent reentries to the double-support phase, the toes of the thrower's right foot should make contact with the ground near his left heel.

• Make sure the thrower tries to keep the right foot back on the first turn, to help in keeping the weight on the right foot.

• During the competitive season, have your throwers concentrate on only one drill a day. Stress to them that learning the drills will help them develop their throws.

AFTERWORD

by Jim Santos and Ken Shannon

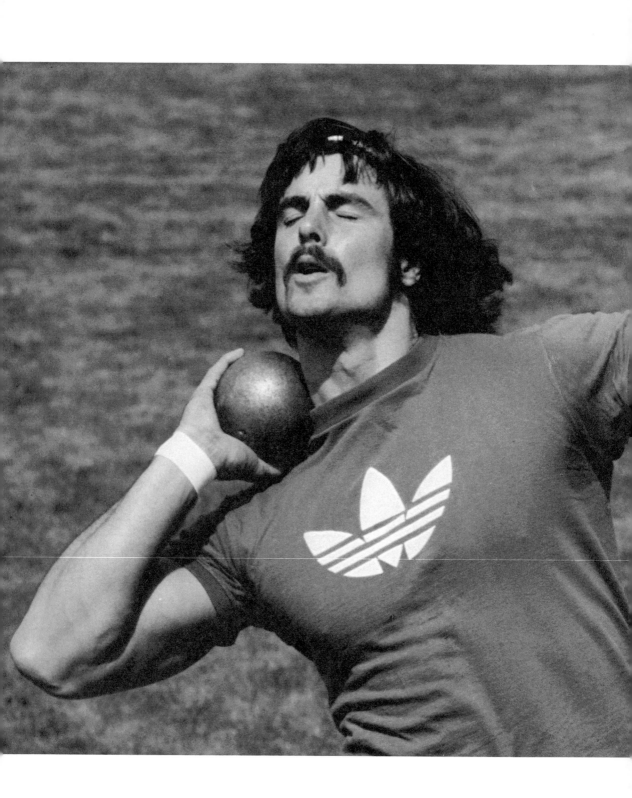

Some Thoughts on Success in the Field Events

What is the secret to success? To self-confidence? To productivity? What is the difference between a winner and the rest of the pack? Dennis Waitley, in his book *The Winner's Edge,* states that a winner is not the product of a privileged environment or a high I.Q., a superior education, or unusual talent. Nor is he or she a matter of luck! The key to success is simply attitude. It is up to coaches to set an example while helping their athletes work on the three ingredients for a successful attitude:

1. *Be honest with yourself.* Assume responsibility for your actions. You must take the credit or blame for your place in life. Our rewards depend entirely on our contributions! As an athlete this involves hard work, correct diet, enough rest for a disciplined schedule, and more. Be committed to your future, and start to consider the precise relationship of athletics to your overall life. Do you enjoy track and field? Good for you. But don't let other aspects of your life—particularly your education—founder as you pursue an athletic dream. Do your best at both. Give your best to each.

2. *Find your own gifts and then follow your own goals.* Live according to your own deepest convictions and abilities, daring to be different yet respecting the rights of others. How will you know you've made the right choice? We believe that being committed to something such as track and field can help teach the passion and discipline required to help make a proper career choice! As running and throwing teach us every day: Do we ever know until we try?

3. *Be able to adapt, and most important, be able to adapt to stress.* A failure to adapt to stress has become the main cause for depression and drug and alcohol abuse in our society. We must be able to learn how to tolerate stress and not try to escape from it. Dennis Waitely advises that we must learn to

Successful throwers and jumpers are honest about their talents, set realistic goals, and through self-discipline and hard work, achieve what they visualize for themselves.

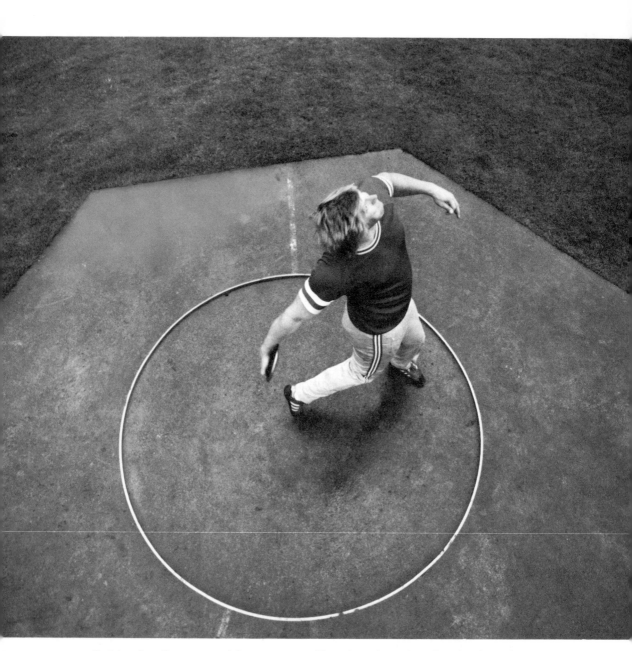

Outstanding throwers and jumpers are self-motivated, goal-setting, hardworking, and realistic about their talents. Off the field, these traits serve them well in other endeavors.

accept the many stresses in our lives and view them as corrective feedback. This
can be painful, but escapism is no answer.

Get control of your life.

Do not try to escape from reality.

Athletics in general, and track and field in particular, can be one of the greatest teachers about life and how to cope with it. In track and field, you are on your own; you cannot rely on a teammate to cover your mistakes in competition. Only you can perform for yourself; no one else can perform for you. A quality track-and-field experience can teach you:

- *Goal setting*—progressing from one level of excellence to the next.
- *Self-discipline*—learning to set standards for yourself in order to achieve your goals. This involves establishing training cycles, skill improvement tests, a regular daily training schedule, and a vision for what you wish to achieve.
- *A sense of reality*—coupled with an ability to dream a little. See yourself throwing the perfect throw; see yourself as a team captain, a school record holder, a state champion, an Olympic team member, or—yes, the ultimate—an Olympic gold medalist.
- *A sense of hard work.* You have your plan; now how do you execute it? Simply by going to practice every day, doing your best, and working hard.

A quality track-and-field experience can also inspire in you a desire for a college education. And it can help you find a career, because it teaches you so much about yourself, particularly how you can depend on yourself.

Do you know what an affirmation is? An affirmation is a positive statement about yourself that may not be true when you make it, but indicates something you wish to be. It is our hope that you are now ready to make an affirmation to become a better jumper, thrower, or coach. The successful athletes we have coached all made affirmations of one kind or another at different stages in their careers. No doubt they are still making them today. Some have gone on to become doctors, teachers, scientists, lawyers, or engineers, and track and field helped them in the pursuit of their careers because it taught them to seek excellence in themselves, and it taught them discipline. No matter what future you desire for yourself, you must learn to be totally committed if you are to succeed! Track and field can help teach you this commitment, and we hope this book is a useful resource in your progress toward your highest goals.